Using Creative Arts-Based Research Methods in School Settings

This book considers the practical challenges likely to be faced when conducting research in the reality of busy educational contexts. It presents an understanding of the perceived efficacy and accessibility of creative research approaches from the perspective of participants as well as the researcher. The book addresses key concerns in research that seeks to understand children's experiences in terms of creativity in thinking, methods and analysis, the school setting as a socially constructed environment, and power relations in experience and data production.

Written in an accessible style that provides a representation of the evolution of arts-based research methods, it includes illustrative case studies, practical suggestions and guidance on further reading. This book will assist higher education researchers seeking to represent subjective experience and empower participants in the creative research process.

This book will be vital reading for researchers completing projects within primary and secondary school settings, as well as those involved in teaching and studying at postgraduate level within MA Education programmes. It will also be of interest to students of research methods at undergraduate level.

Suzanne Everley is Head of Sport Social Science and Reader in the Sociology of Physical Education, Activity and Health at the University of Chichester, UK.

Using Creative Arts-Based Research Methods in School Settings

Understanding and Empowering Children and Young People

Suzanne Everley

LONDON AND NEW YORK

First published 2021
by Routledge
2 Park Square, Milton Park, Abingdon, Oxon OX14 4RN

and by Routledge
52 Vanderbilt Avenue, New York, NY 10017

Routledge is an imprint of the Taylor & Francis Group, an informa business

© 2021 Suzanne Everley

The right of Suzanne Everley to be identified as author of this work has been asserted by her in accordance with sections 77 and 78 of the Copyright, Designs and Patents Act 1988.

All rights reserved. No part of this book may be reprinted or reproduced or utilised in any form or by any electronic, mechanical, or other means, now known or hereafter invented, including photocopying and recording, or in any information storage or retrieval system, without permission in writing from the publishers.

Trademark notice: Product or corporate names may be trademarks or registered trademarks, and are used only for identification and explanation without intent to infringe.

British Library Cataloguing-in-Publication Data
A catalogue record for this book is available from the British Library

Library of Congress Cataloging-in-Publication Data
Names: Everley, Suzanne, author.
Title: Using creative arts-based research methods in school settings : understanding and empowering children and young people / Suzanne Everley.
Description: Abingdon, Oxon ; New York, NY : Routledge, 2021. | Includes bibliographical references and index.
Identifiers: LCCN 2020048801 (print) | LCCN 2020048802 (ebook) | ISBN 9781138089402 (hardback) | ISBN 9781138089440 (paperback) | ISBN 9781315109206 (ebook)
Subjects: LCSH: Education--Research--Methodology. | Creative thinking in children. | Creative ability in adolescence. | School environment--Research--Methodology. | Education, Primary--Research--Methodology. | Education, Secondary--Research--Methodology.
Classification: LCC LB1028 .E9143 2021 (print) | LCC LB1028 (ebook) | DDC 370.72--dc23
LC record available at https://lccn.loc.gov/2020048801
LC ebook record available at https://lccn.loc.gov/2020048802

ISBN: 978-1-138-08940-2 (hbk)
ISBN: 978-1-138-08944-0 (pbk)
ISBN: 978-1-315-10920-6 (ebk)

Typeset in Bembo
by Taylor & Francis Books

To my children, Alexia and Lucca – you are my inspiration
In memory of my father, Alexander Groves, 1930–2020

Contents

List of illustrations		viii
Acknowledgements		ix
1	Introduction	1
2	Why use creative approaches in education research?	14
3	Selecting tools for creative research	30
4	Generating viable data	55
5	The nature of power and empowerment	71
6	Interpretation and analysis	88
7	Research sensitivities and reflections	108
	Index	123

Illustrations

Figures

2.1	The composition of creative thinking in research	17
2.2	Using language with pictures	18
2.3	Using pictures with language	19
2.4	Essential features of creative tools in research with children	20
2.5	Conceptualising 'richness of data': dichotomies of significance	23
3.1	Drama as 'cool' (Kelly, aged 14yrs)	34
3.2	Simple social mapping	35
3.3	Molly's representation of her leadership programme (aged 14yrs)	39
3.4	Hierarchies in school (Jessie, aged 14yrs)	41
3.5	Joseph's representation of himself in a 'You-Cube' (aged 7yrs)	45
3.6	'Me at school' (Tom, aged 6yrs)	46
3.7	'Me at school' (Jeremy, aged 5yrs)	46
3.8	Charlie's sandbox of groups of children in her class	47
4.1	Ensuring product viability	56
5.1	The vulnerable child and the research process – considerations for the researcher	73
5.2	Kyle's captioned picture submitted in lieu of his own drawing (aged 14yrs)	81
6.1	Data sets for children in school	91
6.2	The process of generating your data set	92
6.3	Dimensional model for analysis of children's data sets	93
6.4	Marisa's picture of herself with her bike (aged 7yrs)	94
6.5	Representation of friendship (Michael, aged 14yrs)	96
6.6	Marisa's full picture (aged 7yrs)	97
6.7	An overview of the analytic and interpretive processes	103
7.1	Identifying and utilising assumptions through reflexive processes	112
7.2	The reflexive process	114

Acknowledgements

I would like to thank all of the children and teachers who have worked with me on my research and the students whose stories have been shared here. Thanks also to my husband Keith for his continued support and proof-reading over the years.

Chapter 1

Introduction

The evolution of creative approaches to research, and research with children, has been significant in recent years, and the two are very often considered to be closely aligned. This, however, is sometimes derived from assumptions that children are 'naturally' artistic or creative in thought and will necessarily have a close affinity with such approaches. Much research with children is also conducted within school settings as convenient environments. However, there is significantly more than simple facilitating factors that support the use of creativity in research, studies with children and the impact of these being completed within a school setting. This book explores, in detail, the justifications and practicalities of how effective research can be carried out with children in school in order to understand their lifeworlds and the implications of this.

Creative approaches to research are now an accepted branch of social sciences, and qualitative research more generally across a range of disciplines. They involve divergent thinking as process and product in an endeavour to represent complexities of experience and generate new knowledge forms. It is a dynamic field of research that continues to evolve on the basis of its relationship with cultural practices. The nature of creativity is a complex phenomenon: this text will consider how it operates within research processes (ways of approaching a research question at different stages), methodologies (the rationale behind the research design in light of the research problem), methods (as in the tools that are utilised) and analysis (as interpretive orientation).

The evolving nature of this branch of research forms an essential part of the considerations here and emphasis is placed on the wide range of possibilities that creative approaches offer. Taking research methods as an example, the tools focused on here are characterised by involving the generation of an artefact that is representative of a participant's experience, such as in visual research methods. On this basis, the iterations of children and young people's expression alters over time, and carries with it cultural sensitivities. This applies not only to those tools that may be used, but also to the meaning that these can have in, and of, themselves for participants. To illustrate: when I began using photography with young people in research, this form of expression was exceptional to activities that children would ordinarily be asked to engage in. Now, however, for many children in western contexts, taking photographs is an integral part of culture. This therefore suggests that the meaning of engaging in this process has significantly changed and affects how they might be used to explore research questions.

Turning to the place of this book, many publications of research with children have been criticised for placing an emphasis on discussion of theory rather than methodology (Allan & Tinkler, 2015). There have also long been warnings against the ways in which utilising theory in more traditional forms of research can result in a tendency to prejudice researchers to find particular 'facts' in the data they are working with (Guba and Lincoln, 1989). This text concerns research design and methodology that is rationalised on the centralisation of children's voices in research. This can address research questions through theory generation, such as in a grounded theory approach, or still test theory, but by prioritising children's perspectives. In order to achieve this, the concept of creativity is not limited to the processes that participants may engage in when you conduct your research – it can also involve your own way of thinking creatively as a researcher and responding to data, thus supporting the realisation of the emancipatory potential of research with children through finding complex ways of understanding subjective experience (Everley, 2019).

Conducting research within school settings is sometimes something that happens for convenience rather than being fully rationalised in light of research questions. This can be, to some degree, justifiable on a superficial level; if you are interested in education then it makes sense to conduct research in school, as this is where experiences are taking place. However, it is also often a place of convenience in that children as a participant group are accessible within a safeguarded environment, rather than being understood in terms of the impact that the school as a location has on data collection.

As a result, in many instances, the school itself can be rendered neutralised in representation within research. However, schools are highly politicised environments both in terms of institutional and organisational practices, and also within the socio-cultural relations of children as individuals and groups. On many levels, schools are dialectically constructed, relational spaces that impact children's experiences, both in view of topics that may be being addressed in research and also in terms of the ways in which research may be conducted within such environments. This text, therefore, considers how the concept of space and place affects your work as a researcher, and how this might be managed in school-based investigations.

The purpose of this book is to address key concerns in research that seeks to understand children's experiences in terms of:

a   Creativity in thinking, methods and analysis
b   The school setting as a socially constructed environment
c   Power relations in experience and data production

These are themes that will appear throughout the text. On a practical level, creative approaches in schools are challenging. To support meeting the demands of this, I draw on examples from literature and present illustrations from my own work that I hope will help you maximise the efficacy of your research design in reflecting children's experiences as closely as possible.

Research with children

To establish why research with children and young people requires distinct consideration as compared to other forms of investigation, it is potentially helpful to explore how we have arrived at this point. Thinking about my own research journey, I began publishing research with children in the late 1990s, and would then preface my arguments on the basis that children have lacked representation in research of any meaningful kind. As I shared my research at conferences this seemed to be seen as a relatively novel 'idea' (and therefore 'good'), as it was considered democratising to seek representation of 'child voice'.

However, over time I began to be challenged in terms of what value there was to the children in my conducting research with them as participants (which raised the question of who am I representing them to, for what purpose, and what is the outcome for the children themselves anyway). Concerns were expressed as to whether the practices underpinning my approach were, in a sense, consistent with a concern articulated by Gallacher and Gallagher (2008) that children required my empowerment in order to enact change. I was therefore in danger of perpetuating the kind of relationship that I was aiming to contest. This was at a point where the centralisation of children as active participants in research was advancing significantly in its sophistication, and being impacted by wider policy change that affected the place of children in society (Gormally & Coburn, 2014). We were seeing a development from speaking about 'child voice' to more specifically listening to 'children's voices', recognising the multiplicity of perspectives that can be represented (Lomax, 2012). However, a concern for me now is that it is still almost the norm for authors working with children to begin their papers by establishing an argument on the basis that children's voices are (still) not heard in research. It is argued that children's experiences in education are (still) notable by their absence (Torre & Murphy, 2015).

To summarise the place of children in research, initially they were considered a population upon which research needs to be conducted – i.e., the child seen as an 'object' of investigation. This idea then progressed to one where, in the late seventies, children were seen to have the potential to express their perceptions assessing their own social and cultural condition (see, for example, the work of Apple, 1979) – i.e., being the 'subject' and being seen as competent constructors of their own social condition (Freeman & Mathison, 2008; Gallacher & Gallagher, 2008; Lipponen, Rajala, Hilppö, & Paananen, 2016; Sanderud, 2020). We are now at a point where they can be regarded as experts in their own lives (Aldridge, 2014; Clark, 2017; Lipponen et al., 2016; Vaswani, 2018).

Even through the period when there was evident progress shown from engaging with children more productively in the research process, there were still criticisms that researchers were entering the field with a tendency to converge evidence into that of their own preconceived 'answers' they believed children would give (Apple, 1979). Such concerns still exist now in expressions that vulnerable groups, to which children in school belong, are still represented through adult filters (Martin, Burbach, Lares Benitez, & Ramiz, 2019). Nevertheless, it is possible that children can be included as 'participants' in the active construction of knowledge if research approaches are adequately designed (Gallacher & Gallagher, 2008; Vaswani, 2018).

The evolution from being marginalised in, or absent from, research is reflective of the emphasis in social science research on children as having something to say about their current condition, rather than only being seen in terms of what they may become, which has been arguably a persistent problem within studies of the sociology of childhood (Gallacher & Gallagher, 2008; Lipponen et al., 2016). Such a paradigm shift is effectively mandated through the UN convention on the rights of the child (Aldridge, 2012), which legislates that children have the right to be consulted in issues that affect them (Everley, 2018), and now forms a key consideration in research design and justification. Children are now seen as holders of rights (Clark, 2017; Swartz, 2011), and this has redefined the way that they are accounted for in research. This text seeks to consider how creative approaches to research can work with children in exercising such rights, enabling expression of personal expertise and exploring how we inform our endeavours to understand the 'voices' of children.

Creative methods and knowledge generation

Essential to understanding children's experience is their involvement as participants in the production of knowledge about them (Lomax, 2012; Swartz, 2011). So, if we are to extend the representation of children and young people's voices, we need to utilise ways of researching that: reflect the complexities of their experiences, and employ means of communication that are malleable in the expression of nuanced perception and that can be seen as academically rigorous.

Creatively based forms of research can address a range of research questions and are not narrowed to apply only to one kind of epistemological perspective (McCaffrey & Edwards, 2015). However, this text does assume that whatever research question is being explored, we are interested in understanding children's subjective experiences. This is essentially a phenomenological positioning wherein we are concerned with perception and meaning. Every individual will be selective in their responses to a particular situation, and will experience that situation differently (Shibutani, 1955). This ultimately results in giving individualised meanings to experience. Since it is meanings that guide actions and frame future experiences (Blumer, 1969), and can index how something is experienced, understanding this can ultimately be used to anticipate how any change as a result of research might be received.

Therefore, within creative research with children we are prioritising the participant's perspective (Giguere, 2011). Although some authors have questioned whether children are necessarily in the best position to understand themselves (Gallacher & Gallagher, 2008; Lomax, 2012), it is only they who know how they experience particular phenomena. Since children will act on what they think is happening, rather than necessarily what seems to be happening from the perspective of the external observer, finding the best way to understand this could generate new knowledge in research.

What do we need to know and how can we come to know it?

Prior to beginning research, it is helpful to think carefully about what knowledge actually 'is' (this being an ontological perspective) and how we might come to know it (this being the epistemological perspective). In terms of researching with children, what follows in this book is predicated on the belief that knowledge is made up of multiple realities (i.e., children's experiences of a research question will be different but will share some commonalities that can be identified). It assumes that we can come to know this by using creative approaches to research that enable children to define their own response to a research question without any pre-categorisation of points of interest being specified by the researcher.

This type of research, therefore, has an 'emic' ontological perspective (as opposed to 'etic', which presupposes that there is a single reality to be discovered). We are therefore also saying that understanding what can be known is specific to particular situations and individuals (Lincoln & Guba, 1985). To do this, we need to find a way of facilitating the expression of experience and ensure differentiated understanding of meaning for children (Mannay, Staples, & Edwards, 2017).

As young children tend to communicate using a range of senses (Clark, 2017), and older children are likely to engage through the use of tools that are culturally normative, it would seem to be logical to incorporate ways of engaging with children that are consistent with these. This is also aligned with a general shift in what is considered acceptable in research, away from previous privileging of communication in formal language (Bridger, 2013). On a personal level, this is also in response to the ways in which children I have worked with engaged in particular research methods. The first indication of the possibilities of non-language-based communication came, for me, when children kept journals about a particular topic but included drawings, either for emphasis or to replace language. This led me to explore the use of drawings as a research tool with children; this work was based on the theoretical perspectives of the value of drawings in arts therapy and was well grounded in understanding their perspectives. However, when children completed drawings in research for me, there still appeared to be a need for words in some instances, as subsequent exploration of drawings as a tool demonstrated that words or comments would be added to ensure a particular meaning was conveyed. What this began to make clear was the need to think more creatively about how more than one means of conveying meaning may be the most appropriate way forward in research with children. In terms of thinking creatively about how best to understand perspectives, it is also possible to employ more artistic means of completing every phase of research. This includes, as recommended by McCaffrey & Edwards (2015), in the analysis of data.

The purposes of this book

This book explores creative approaches to research and aims to illustrate how these can be used to cast experience in some kind of material form in order for us to be open to new knowledge about children's perspectives. Freeman and Mathison (2008), for example, suggest that drawings can be a means through which children can bring order to their experiences. Other methods used with children have similarly involved arts-based work using photography, mapping and collage (Allan & Tinkler, 2015; Lomax, 2012; Viega, 2016). Creative approaches to research can include all of these activities, and the tools discussed here always include an active production of data by children (Gallacher & Gallagher, 2008). However, as alluded to above, and as will be discussed, creativity as an approach to research involves not only the tools that we select, but also the way we think about and approach research. Here, it is hoped that I will be able to illustrate the relationship between this and the nature of understanding experience. What I suggest is that being inclusive in research, i.e. involving children, is not in itself sufficient to represent voices. Consideration of a host of factors that have adjunct roles is required in order to create a genuinely enabling environment. In particular, spacial considerations that are so often missing in research (Anderson, Adey, & Bevan, 2010) will be addressed.

What this book also hopes to do is discuss these considerations in both theoretical and practical ways. The completion of research is rarely straightforward and the school environment, despite being ordered in many ways, can be hugely unpredictable. To this end, I will share thoughts drawn from experience in the field, as practical considerations can significantly affect research (Munro, Holmes, & Ward, 2005). I will also highlight some of the potential challenges that it may be helpful to be aware of. I also acknowledge that 'so-called' child-friendly methods (Gallacher & Gallagher, 2008) will not always be accessible to the children that you want to include in your research.

As identified above, and unsurprisingly, much research regarding children has been conducted within school settings, yet very little has attended to the particulars of the role of the environment – social, cultural and physical – as it impacts on research, in terms of the identification of research problems, design of studies and how these are conducted in practice. It is the purpose of this book to address, in a practical way, questions that you may have regarding making authentic representations of school children and young people's experiences, in order to support you through the research process and beyond. There is no perfect way of designing your research when you work in a school environment – things will not go as planned and there will be any number of factors that will seem to sabotage your work. Research in schools will be 'messy' and unpredictable (Flanagan, 2012) but, by the same token, it will be stimulating, challenging and hugely valuable as we all work towards a better understanding of the perspectives of children and young people.

How to use this book

Within this text I use the term children to refer to participants aged 4–16yrs as those that we are most likely to meet in a school setting. There will be some points at which a distinction is made to refer to older children (those of secondary school age, 11–16yrs) where I will more specifically refer to 'young people'. Where discussing children of primary school age (4–11yrs) I refer to 'younger children'. With careful consideration of your own position as researcher, the particular school and group/individuals that you are working with, the majority of concepts discussed here can be applied across age ranges.

I consider that the work here will support you in the representation of children's *voices*, as this conceptualisation indicates that you may be interpreting a multiplicity of perspectives to represent a whole or enabling your research to attend to the 'n = 1' of distinct experience of individuals where appropriate. Each chapter has a particular focus but is related to others – it is therefore possible for you to select a particular subject that you want to learn about, although you will be directed to other points in the book that may be useful in support of this.

The following chapter begins by considering what we actually mean by creative approaches to research and explores why we might use them. Consideration is given to your own creative thinking as a researcher, being creative in research design, and how this relates to ways of exploring and identifying new knowledge. The relationship that such an approach has with children's culture is also examined with the associations between the production of artefacts and accessing meaning being considered. Tools of engagement are addressed in Chapter 3. Here there is a focus on the practicalities of what you can do with children in their expression of their subjective experiences. The relative advantages of different tools in creative expression are considered. Discussion focuses largely on visual research methods, although other creative tools that may be of value in the research process are also referred to. Chapter 4 focuses on how we can ensure that our data is viable – i.e. that creates data that warrants, and is manageable in, analysis. Power 'distribution' and its relationship with your action as adult researcher with participants as children is addressed in Chapter 5. Practical means of analysing data are explored in Chapter 6, before Chapter 7 concludes with considerations of sensitising yourself to, and within, school as a physical, social and cultural research setting, and the use of reflection and reflexion both during, and following, your investigation.

Each chapter includes 'scenarios' that have been taken from research situations that may help you interpret the main text and/or consider how key points might apply to your own research context. 'Thinking points' identify questions that you may ask yourself to support addressing the issues that are included in the discussion, and an overview of ethical considerations related to the key focus of the chapter are explored. Children's involvement in research is regarded to bring its own particular set of ethical considerations (Powell et al., 2018; Richardson, 2019). Conducting ethical research with children should be a constantly reviewed process; this will form part of more formalised requirements to a greater or lesser extent. This text will identify the range of considerations that you may need to make in terms of each aspect of the research process, with particular reference to the more nuanced challenges of moral rights that may emerge as you progress.

Gaining initial ethical approval

As identified above, each chapter of this text will address particular ethical questions and dilemmas that may arise during your work. There are, however, specific points of ethical approval that it will be assumed you have obtained prior to the commencement of your study. In terms of general ethical considerations that you will make here, these will be dependent upon the expectations of your particular institution or other body responsible for assessing the ethical risk of your work. Your own organisation's ethics committee will have key responsibility in approving your proposal and ensuring standards (Brown, Spiro, & Quinton, 2020). Therefore, your work will be a balance between obligations as set, and the intentions of your research (Slepičková & Bartošová, 2014). What you will be establishing is ethically managed research that treats your child participants as both informed and competent (Darian-Smith & Henningham, 2014).

In the first instance, there is a need to gain ethically secure access through adults responsible for potential child participants (Arnott, Martinez-Lejarreta, Wall, Blaisdell, & Palaiologou, 2020). Such individuals are ordinarily regarded as 'gatekeepers' within the research process (Powell et al., 2018; Richardson, 2019). Very often, these agents constitute a hierarchy that requires navigation before you reach the children that you hope to involve in your work (Sendil & Sonmez, 2020).

With respect to working in schools, this will include the headteacher, in the first instance, and any teachers or other adults that you are working with within that environment. These key individuals will need to give informed consent permitting you to proceed with your work. Here it is important to ensure that the consent is formalised through written agreements, but also that it is personally, genuinely supported by all involved. Having the investment of significant figures within school can also make an enormous difference to the quality of research that you carry out. The data you are likely to be able to generate when working with children will depend on the environment that is set up within the school on your behalf, if you are a visitor, or with you if you are already working/training in the school. There is likely to be limited benefit to your work if staff feel under pressure from a headteacher to facilitate your study. Similarly, there is no purpose in having an enthusiastic staff but a headteacher who does not support what you are seeking to achieve. Such ethical considerations, therefore, are not only a moral obligation but of practical value to your research.

It is, therefore, important to ensure that you establish good communications with all adults that may be affected by the research. Setting up research with children necessarily involves the detailed negotiation and building of relationships (Powell et al., 2018). If working in a school it is likely that you have some personal connection in the first instance that can support this process. This is a good basis on which to have an informal conversation about your proposal to gauge how individuals may feel about it. If you do not already know those you would like to be involved, and you are arriving as an outsider (Mortari & Harcourt, 2012), then asking for an informal meeting (preferably face to face if possible) to discuss your research design can help address any concerns that adults working with the children may have. It would be advisable that these open discussions are held with all who are likely to be involved before you begin to engage in any formalities regarding gaining ethical approval. This will clearly also begin to establish relationships upon which your fieldwork will actually be based.

Although processes may vary, the next stage of your work will usually involve gaining consent from parents to allow their children to be involved in your work. It is important to be mindful here that this is very much a 'first stage' in selecting your participants. This will involve sending an information sheet and consent form to parents/guardians of the children that you would hope to involve in your work. The information sheet would need to outline who you are, the purposes of the study and exactly what children will, or may be, asked to do as a participant in it. It is also helpful to include details of the benefits to the children themselves, their parents and/or the school, that may be derived from their involvement. Reference ordinarily needs to be made to give assurances of anonymity, the right to withdraw without question (along with dates as to when this would need to happen) and to strongly emphasise that taking part is voluntary to the child (BERA, 2018). It needs to be written in an accessible, concise way to ensure respondents genuinely understand what is involved.

With respect to the consent form itself, depending on the levels of sensitivity of your topic of investigation, it is possible that this can be done on an 'opt out' or 'opt in' basis. Here, the latter can be hugely helpful when addressing issues that are anticipated to not be sensitive. This is with respect to the realities of dealing with communications to parents, particularly if you are anticipating conducting research on specific dates with children in groups. Regarding this, if asking parents to return permission slips, it is not unusual to find that children who really want to take part, and whose parent or guardian are happy for them to do so, have forgotten the response that confirms this. In such an instance, you will not be able to include such children in what you are doing. In these cases, structuring your ethical approval around the assumptions that parents will return a response to a letter only if they do *not* want their child to participate, means you avoid this problem. Nevertheless, this is to be done with a note of caution, as it is possible a return should have come to you identifying that permissions are not given but did not arrive. Indeed, many schools no longer support taking this approach. Therefore, if you are seeking active permission for participants to engage in your study, you need to ensure that letters are sent to parents/guardians (whether a physical or electronic communication using the school systems) well ahead of the point at which you need to conduct your study. This will allow you to send polite reminders for return slips to be completed. Giving a submission 'deadline' that still allows for you to follow up any delayed returns after this is also advisable.

The final, and crucially important, point of informed consent concerns the children that you wish to be involved in your study. The way that you manage this will be very dependent upon the age and maturity of your intended participants. The concept of children giving consent does have its tensions (Arnott et al., 2020), and there is a degree of irony that even where they are at the centre of the research, their permissions can only be sought at the end of the hierarchical processes described above. This also means that there may be instances where children have already been prevented from joining the research by others that have been consulted before them (Sendil & Sonmez, 2020).

Nevertheless, if you can reach a point where you can directly seek the consent of children, this needs to be actively achieved (Hammersley, 2015). Again, you will need to ask for participants to indicate that they have fully understood what your study is about, what they are being asked to do to be part of it, how their data will be used, and that they are happy to join in. This means you will need to use age appropriate language and ensure that the points you highlight are understood by the children you are inviting to join your project. For example, saying that you are completing an undergraduate/postgraduate dissertation may not be meaningful to your potential participants, but identifying that you are at university conducting a study that aims to learn more about a particular topic in order to help teachers in school, may be.

An additional thought here also is whether children are of an age and understanding to be able to give 'consent'. If it is the case that they are not, then it may be more appropriate to use an assent form where you explain the very basics of what you are investigating and what the children are being asked to do. As a form of agreement that acknowledges children cannot demonstrate *complete* understanding, assent does not have the legal standing that consent does. However, it is indicative of genuine endeavour to ensure children understand the nature and purposes of research as far as possible (Oulton et al., 2016). On a most basic level, it is indicative of aquiescence to being involved (Arnott et al., 2020). In each of these cases it is advisable, as a minimum, to include a verbal explanation and create a genuine opportunity for your participants to ask questions. It is also hugely important that when you identify that there is no requirement to be, or remain, part of your study, that this is done on a genuine basis so that children feel able to express this (Graham, Powell, & Taylor, 2015; Hammersley, 2015). Give children assurances that if they do not want to join you, or change their mind about doing so, they genuinely understand this is the case. It is also important to remember that if a child does not wish to take part, then their position supersedes any permissions that may have been given by parents/guardians. Although it is possible to have some instances where children would not want to be anonymous (Graham et al., 2015) ordinarily, as described above, giving assurances of anonymity and confidentiality is both a presumed, and explicit, expectation of your approach.

Although specific considerations pertaining to each chapter are discussed in relation to the points above, an assumption throughout this book is that you will have some concept of essential ethical considerations that are involved in any research with children. Therefore, the purpose of the ethical discussions that are included in each chapter of this text is not so much to guide you as to what permissions you may require, but to broaden your thinking about what ethical considerations might need to be made with reference to the practicalities of actually conducting your research in school. Therefore, although ethical approval will need to be obtained before you begin your study, ethical considerations should be considered to underpin every aspect of your research as you carry it out. As these are themselves considered an essential informant of creative approaches to research, the next chapter turns to address what we mean by such approaches, and how these provide a basis for research thinking, processes and outcomes.

References

Aldridge, J. (2012). The participation of vulnerable children in photographic research. *Visual Studies*, 27(1), 48–58.

Aldridge, J. (2014). Working with vulnerable groups in social research: dilemmas by default and design. *Qualitative Research*, 14(1), 112–130.

Allan, A., & Tinkler, P. (2015). 'Seeing' into the past and 'looking' forward to the future: visual methods and gender and education research. *Gender & Education*, 27(7), 791–811. doi:10.1080/09540253.2015.1091919.

Anderson, J., Adey, P., & Bevan, P. (2010). Positioning place: polylogic approaches to research methodology. *Qualitative Research*, 10(5), 589–604.

Apple, M. (1979). *Ideology and Curriculum*. London: Routledge and Kegan Paul.

Arnott, L., Martinez-Lejarreta, L., Wall, K., Blaisdell, C., & Palaiologou, I. (2020). Reflecting on three creative approaches to informed consent with children under six. *British Educational Research Journal*, 46(4), 786–810. doi:10.1002/berj.3619.

BERA (2018). *Ethical Guidelines for Educational Research*, 4th ed.

Blumer, H. (1969). *Symbolic Interactionism - Perspective and Method*. Englewood Cliffs, NJ: Prenctice-Hall.

Bridger, L. (2013). Seeing and telling households: a case for photo elicitation and graphic elicitation in qualitative research. *Graduate Journal of Social Science*, 10(2), 106–131.

Brown, C., Spiro, J., & Quinton, S. (2020). The role of research ethics committees: friend or foe in educational research? An exploratory study. *British Educational Research Journal*, 46(4), 747–769. doi:10.1002/berj.3654.

Clark, A. (2017). *Listening to Young Children: A Guide to Understanding and Using the Mosaic Approach*. Expanded 3rd ed. London: Jessica Kingsley Publishers.

Darian-Smith, K., & Henningham, N. (2014). Social research and the privacy and participation of children: reflections on researching Australian children's playlore. *Children & Society*, (4), 327. doi:10.1111/j.1099-0860.2012.00475.x.

Everley, S. (2019). Using visual research tools when working with children in a primary school setting. In R. Medcalfe and C. Mackintosh (Eds.), *Researching Difference in Sport and Physical Activity* (pp. 55–70). London and New York: Routledge.

Flanagan, P. (2012). Ethical review and reflexivity in research of children's sexuality. *Sex Education*, 12(5), 535–544. doi:10.1080/14681811.2011.627731.

Freeman, M., & Mathison, S. (2008). *Researching Children's Experiences*. New York: Guilford Publications.

Gallacher, L. A., & Gallagher, M. (2008). Methodological immaturity in childhood research? Thinking through 'participatory methods', *Childhood*, 15(4), 499–516.

Giguere, M. (2011). Social influences on the creative process: an examination of children's creativity and learning in dance. *International Journal of Education & the Arts*, 12(1).

Gormally, S., & Coburn, A. (2014). Finding Nexus: connecting youth work and research practices. *British Educational Research Journal*, 40(5), 869–885. doi:10.1002/berj.3118.

Graham, A., Powell, M. A., & Taylor, N. (2015). Ethical research involving children. *Family Matters*, (96), 23–28.

Guba, E., & Lincoln, Y. (1989). *Fourth Generation Evaluation Newbury Park*. CA: Sage Publications.

Hammersley, M. (2015). Research ethics and the concept of children's rights. *Children & Society*, 29(6), 569–582. doi:10.1111/chso.12077.

Lincoln, Y. S. & Guba, E. G. (1985). *Naturalistic Inquiry*. Newbury Park, CA: Sage Publications.

Lipponen, L., Rajala, A., Hilppö, J., & Paananen, M. (2016). Exploring the foundations of visual methods used in research with children. *European Early Childhood Education Research Journal*, 24(6), 936–946. doi:10.1080/1350293X.2015.1062663.

Lomax, H. (2012). Contested voices? Methodological tensions in creative visual research with children. *International Journal of Social Research Methodology*, 15(2), 105–117. doi:10.1080/13645579.2012.649408.

Mannay, D., Staples, E., & Edwards, V. (2017). Visual methodologies, sand and psychoanalysis: employing creative participatory techniques to explore the educational experiences of mature students and children in care. *Visual Studies*, 32(4), 345–358. doi:10.1080/1472586X.2017.1363636.

Martin, S. B., Burbach, J. H., Lares Benitez, L., & Ramiz, I. (2019). Participatory action research and co-researching as a tool for situating youth knowledge at the centre of research. *London Review of Education*, 17(3), 297–313. doi:10.18546/LRE.17.3.05.

McCaffrey, T., & Edwards, J. (2015). Meeting art with art: arts-based methods enhance researcher reflexivity in research with mental health service users. *Journal of Music Therapy*, 52(4), 515–532. doi:10.1093/jmt/thv016.

Mortari, L., & Harcourt, D. (2012). 'Living' ethical dilemmas for researchers when researching with children. *International Journal of Early Years Education*, 20(3), 234–243. doi:10.1080/09669760.2012.715409.

Munro, E. R., Holmes, L., & Ward, H. (2005). Researching vulnerable groups: ethical issues and the effective conduct of research in local authorities. *The British Journal of Social Work*, 35(7), 1023–1038. doi:10.1093/bjsw/bch220.

Oulton, K., Gibson, F., Sell, D., Williams, A., Pratt, L., & Wray, J. (2016). Assent for children's participation in research: why it matters and making it meaningful. *Child: Care, Health & Development*, 42(4), 588–597. doi:10.1111/cch.12344.

Powell, M. A., McArthur, M., Chalmers, J., Graham, A., Moore, T., Spriggs, M., & Taplin, S. (2018). Sensitive topics in social research involving children. *International Journal of Social Research Methodology*, 21(6), 647–660. doi:10.1080/13645579.2018.1462882.

Richardson, T. (2019). 'Why haven't I got one of those?' A consideration regarding the need to protect non-participant children in early years research. *European Early Childhood Education Research Journal*, 27(1), 5–14. doi:10.1080/1350293X.2018.1556530.

Sanderud, J. R. (2020). Mutual experiences: understanding children's play in nature through sensory ethnography. *Journal of Adventure Education & Outdoor Learning*, 20(2), 111–122. doi:10.1080/14729679.2018.1557058.

Sendil, C. O., & Sonmez, S. (2020). Ethics in research including young children: views and experiences of researchers. *Ilkogretim Online*, 19(1), 87–99. doi:10.17051/ilkonline.2020.644821.

Shibutani, T. (1955). Reference groups as perspectives. *American Journal of Sociology*, 60, 562–569.

Slepičková, L., & Bartošová, M. K. (2014). Ethical and methodological associations in doing research on children in a school environment. *New Educational Review*, 38(4), 84–93.

Swartz, S. (2011). 'Going deep' and 'giving back': strategies for exceeding ethical expectations when researching amongst vulnerable youth. *Qualitative Research*, 11(1), 47–68. doi:10.1177/1468794110385885.

Torre, D., & Murphy, J. (2015). A different lens: using photo-elicitation interviews in education research. *Education Policy Analysis Archives*, 23(111), 1–26.

Vaswani, N. (2018). Learning from failure: are practitioner researchers the answer when conducting research on sensitive topics with vulnerable children and young people? *International Journal of Social Research Methodology*, 21(4), 499–512. doi:10.1080/13645579.2018.1434866.

Viega, M. (2016). Science as art: axiology as a central component in methodology and evaluation of arts-based research (ABR). *Music Therapy Perspectives*, 34(1), 4–13.

Chapter 2

Why use creative approaches in education research?

> It was a bit different – doing yourself in pictures – it was like doing a cartoon story – it was more funner than just talking.
>
> (Emily, aged 7yrs)

This chapter presents a rationale as to why we might advocate the use of creative approaches to research in school settings. The discussion assumes a desire to explore children's experiences of phenomena being investigated. It applies to a range of topics but centralises understanding individualised perspectives.

The beliefs of professionals working to develop children's creativity in schools is considered paramount in determining the quality of practice (Maksić & Spasenović, 2018). Similarly, as a researcher, it is important to explore how you interpret the concept and how this will affect what you actually do in your investigations. Although qualitative research is sometimes seen to be creative in and of itself (Konecki, 2019), a much more intentional analysis of what constitutes creativity in research is required to establish purposeful research design. Addressing a phenomenon that is considered highly resistant to conceptualisation (Hammershoj, 2014), this chapter draws on creativity in education theory to consider why we should use such an approach in research.

Key discussion points include the following:

- What constitutes creative approaches to research?
- Creativity as an orientation to research: creative thinking and relevance
- Why use creative tools? Engaging participants
- Why use creative tools? Generation of rich data
- Ethical considerations

I begin by reflecting on what is meant by creative approaches to research, and the implications this has for your research design, behaviours as a researcher, and the actions of your participants within this process.

What constitutes a creative approach to research?

Traditional research methods have, in their design, specifically aimed to avoid creativity, claiming to be value free and independent of context with a focus on what can be considered singular, 'factual' and replicable (Kara, 2015). However, this can be seen as reductive and delimits what can be adequately explored. Additionally, taking any stance in an investigation is necessarily representative of some kind of value system. Since understanding is context dependent and knowledge, interest driven (Zimmerman, 2015), the concept of arguments that purport to offer objective rationalisation are essentially flawed. Indeed, many 'scientific' revelations have often been associated with moments of serendipity for investigators; consider, for example, the discovery of penicillin, pulsars and radioactivity.

This having been said, selection of research approach is dependent upon the topic of investigation and purposes of the study. Being concerned with the experiences of children, what we have is a point of departure that is very deliberately the antithesis of strongly framed, positivist approaches to asking singular questions. Such approaches do not align with seeking to understand perspectives. What creativity brings to research in particular, as discussed in Chapter 1, is an acknowledgement of the complexity of factors that inform children's experiences. To understand how this 'works', it is important to establish what we actually mean by creativity as an ideological and material concept. We need to understand what we mean and how this is realised in practice within research.

To address the constitution of the concept, the notion of creativity will be explored on three levels:

- Creativity in thinking
- Being a creative researcher
- Research tools as both creative process and product

Essentially, the way we think as researchers underpins our selection of approach – therefore, a helpful starting point is to consider what the concept of creative thinking means for you:

> **Thinking points**
>
> How might you answer the following questions based purely on your own experience:
>
> - What do you consider the concept of creativity to be?
> - How do you justify this opinion?
> - Of what use is thinking creatively in the research process?
> - What difference might thinking creatively make to your findings?
> - What effect might this have on the impact of your work?

Perhaps on the most basic level, anything that is original in some sense, either to the individual or wider audiences, can be considered creative (Jeffrey, Craft, & Leibling, 2001). Fautley and Savage (2007) suggest that, by definition, something that is creat*ed* is creat*ive* – this can be both of material and conceptual nature. Considering the latter point, this raises the question of what such conceptualisation may look like for you as a researcher. Formulating creativity cognitively establishes the foundation of research design. In educational research terms, a crucial element of this is the ability to think divergently (Fautley & Savage, 2007; Hanson, 2014). However, to support the process of doing this, utilising some form of material creativity can be helpful. Mapping out the different points of exploration of your research question, for example, may support the realisation of the thought processes that you engage in with respect to thinking about formulating your research problem. This can further develop your thinking about more than what may immediately be apparent, as engaging creatively can help you see problems in different ways (Kara, 2015).

In the context of school-based research, this type of thinking can pertain to three factors. The production of an artefact as representation of meaning, the processes that the individual goes through in order to produce that material outcome, and the interaction through which the researcher might come to interpret and understand the messages that participants want to share. Therefore, creativity can be considered product, process, or both (Fautley & Savage, 2007).

Creativity as an orientation to research: creative thinking and relevance

Thinking divergently, however, is only of value if it is also purposeful. Hammershoj (2014) argues that something considered to be creative is necessarily not only novel, as identified by Jeffrey et al. (2001), but also relevant. The endeavour to move beyond standard ways of knowing (Konecki, 2019) and give rise to new possibilities needs to retain pertinence to your research question. In terms of yourself as a researcher, one aspect of your own creativity may be in terms of your exercise of judgement in relation to the connections between which elements of the experiences being shared with you are relevant and useful – this is the idea of discriminating between elements of the evidence being shared. This conceptualisation is further explored in Chapter 6; where data analysis is discussed, but anticipating how you might make links should inform your thinking at all stages of your study.

With reference to ways in which you might act as a researcher, creativity is not something exclusive but dependent on 'ordinary abilities' of noticing and engaging (Boden, 2010, p261). In terms of educational research, this may be with reference to noticing what has happened, is happening, or reflecting to identify what experiences may have occurred during the research to support new ways of seeing. The 'unanticipated' can therefore be included in your thinking.

This addresses the idea of thinking imaginatively and purposefully to be creative with respect to the artefacts that you may ask children to produce when conducting your research (Fautley & Savage, 2007). This approach to representing experience involves the kind of divergent, purposeful thinking that is being described here. With respect to purposeful, in this particular instance, I refer to the value it has in conveying meaning. As the production of an artefact is also generally 'paced', both you and your participants have time to think carefully about each stage and detail a response as the research progresses, therefore creating analytical opportunities to discern the meaning of what is being produced and how it is being represented, and thus enhancing creative content.

Therefore, to summarise, Figure 2.1 illustrates that thinking creatively in research comprises of three parts: purposeful production, by which we are referring to thinking intentionally about the dimensions of the research question; discernment in relevance, in which thought is pursued in light of its tested pertinence to the research question; and meaningful representation, which involves the configuration of ideas into communicable form. This should ensure that, as research is designed around creative approaches and using creative tools, useable data sets can be generated. Part of this process will be dependent upon the extent to which children engage as participants, and the following section turns to discuss how this can be achieved within this approach.

Why use creative tools? Engaging participants

This section considers the use of creative tools as they exist within the wider concept of creative approaches to research. In research terms of the application we are concerned with here, a 'tool' is a device through which meaning can be communicated. As such, to be creative it needs to present the possibility of generating individualised, complex, and comprehensive data that synthesises the expression of elements of experience.

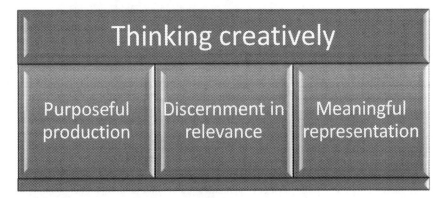

Figure 2.1 The composition of creative thinking in research

18 Why use creative approaches?

Although it is very possible that utilising creative tools in research leads to motivation from enjoyment (Fautley & Savage, 2007), it cannot be assumed that children will necessarily enjoy what they are engaging in (Lomax, 2012). However, the transcendence process in creativity, i.e. the intangible way in which knowledge is transferred from the mind of the child to be presented within an artefact, affects the way that individuals relate to what they are doing (Hammershoj, 2014). As a result, this means that their sense of investment is potentially heightened, and the detail and quality of data generated, enhanced.

What we are seeking in the use of creative tools is the ability to explore different ways of knowing (Fautley & Savage, 2007). Very often, creative tools are considered those that necessarily avoid the need for language – however, whilst such tools are frequently those associated with visual expression, for example with drawings, photographs and dance, they can also include concepts such as journaling or blogging as creative expression through language. Whilst visual alternatives can be helpful where children find it difficult to generate narrative (Mann & Warr, 2017), it does not need to be restricted in this way. Indeed, where one tool is used, children will frequently also incorporate elements of another; for example, where I have used diaries, participants have included drawings, and where I have used drawings they have added words and explanations to their images.

To illustrate, in Figure 2.2, Aisha (aged 14yrs) was asked to draw a representation of herself in PE.

Figure 2.2 Using language with pictures

Why use creative approaches? 19

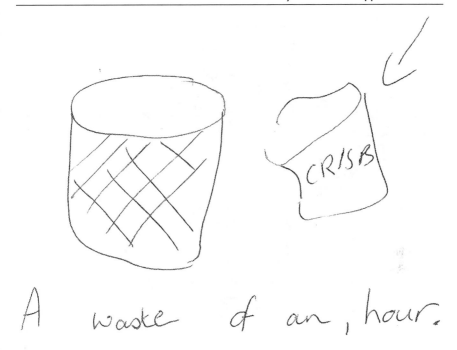

Figure 2.3 Using pictures with language

In Figure 2.3, Clemmie (aged 12yrs) was keeping a diary about her experiences of PE.

Therefore, what matters is not so much the material essence of the tool but its nature in relation to the potential expression of participants. Tool selection therefore needs to be malleable and accessible to children. In addition to this, and significantly in my experience, they should also require investment from the interpreter.

Figure 2.4 maps out features of effective creative research tools. As identified above, when working with children, the idea of using creative approaches is often justified on the basis of being more engaging than other methods of research, since creativity enacts engagement (Fautley & Savage, 2007). However, limited attention has been paid to the value of artefacts in terms of the way children perceive them to be being engaged with by the researcher.

Utilising creative approaches moves us from conducting research on children to conducting research with children (Lipponen, Rajala, Hilppö, & Paananen, 2016). This highlights the investment that children make in these approaches and simultaneously acknowledges the active contribution that forms an essential part of participants' involvement. I would emphasise that, in addition, this can

20 Why use creative approaches?

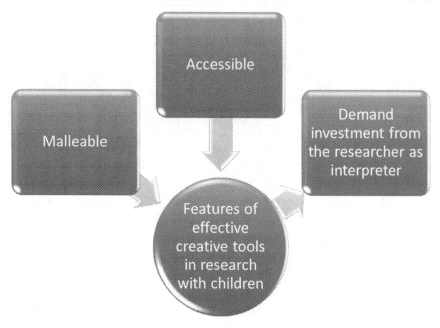

Figure 2.4 Essential features of creative tools in research with children

extend to the active engagement that children that can recognise you as researcher need to demonstrate:

> I think the diaries are good 'cos you can say what you want and you know that the person (researcher) has to actually read it to understand – they've got to kind of join in and try to get into your thinking.
>
> (Carl, aged 15yrs)

Thinking carefully about how you are perceived by your participants is an important part of the research process and considered in more detail in Chapters 4 and 5. The example here clearly illustrates the sense of purpose that can be generated in these research approaches. The anticipated response of the researcher is also what makes data such as photographs 'powerful' (Aldridge, 2012). Therefore, creative approaches by you as a researcher potentially heighten engagement of all involved.

Such orientations can also ensure that children are able to manipulate whichever tool they are using to express a personalised perspective that is representative of their experience. Qualitative methods are generally considered 'fluid', and can therefore allow individualised representations. It is the process of making experience as immaterial (Lipponen et al., 2016), material, and this has the potential to ensure an authenticity of voice that may not be achieved through other methods of research. As you are likely to be seeking representation of perspective and experience, and as these are distinct to the individual (Fautley & Savage, 2007; Liamputtong, 2007), allowing creativity in method can support the expression of complex, personalised stories.

Fautley and Savage have suggested that creativity is motivational when it is pupil led (Fautley & Savage, 2007). From working with children, this is very much the case and, in some instances, when within a research context, engaging with a creative approach is actually motivational for students in itself. As Emily commented:

> It was a bit different – doing yourself in pictures – it was like doing a cartoon story – it was more funner than just talking.
>
> (Emily, aged 7yrs)

This raises the question of potential associations that creative methods can have with children's culture and the value of this, which affects accessibility. Indeed, one of the key reasons for utilising creative approaches in research with children is that it generates the potential to have an association with the culture of childhood and ways in which children may 'naturally' create meaning. Whilst it is necessary to exercise caution in assuming particular activities form part of children's culture, it is reasonable to prioritise that which we think they will positively respond to. Here, an emphasis can be placed both on the way an approach can be meaningful to you as a researcher in answering your question (McCaffrey & Edwards, 2015), and also support the meaningful engagement in research from the perspective of the child. It is worth, also, acknowledging that culture here will refer not only to the artefacts you may be asking children to produce but to the processes through which they may create them (Rose, 2016). Underpinning this is a recognition that, as discussed in Chapter 1, children are not only competent social actors (Lomax, 2012), but that they have the acumen to express consciousness of this through creative cultural means. Therefore, utilising those that are most accessible to children is likely to be more productive for all.

Based on the work of Vygotsky, Lipponen et al. (2016) suggest that experiences themselves are mediated through systems of cultural symbols and artefacts – finding ways of facilitating children's expression through these can be a way of accessing that experience. Thinking about the production of artefacts that children engage in during their everyday lives can help in directing choice of research tool. It is not unusual for younger children to complete drawings as informal gifts, or young people to take photographs to post on social media or send directly to one another. Thinking about these examples we can see not just what artefact production children engage in, but for what purposes they may do so. As with much 'art', the production of the artefact is not always the primary goal (McCaffrey & Edwards, 2015). Considering each of the instances here, this could also be the case – in the instance of the younger child their intention may be to please the recipient; in the case of the older children it may be to impress their peers. Although different forms of creativity emerge at different ages (Hammershoj, 2014), common to each of these examples could be an action to covet approval. Whatever the intention, what we can see is that there are indicators as to how children already use creative means through which to communicate their social worlds, and we can see them as the social actors that they are (Lomax, 2012).

In each of the examples used above, there is arguably an intentional state – whether conscious or otherwise. If we are conducting research with children, these forms of social and cultural practices can help us understand how to access further opportunities to explore children's perspectives (Chesworth, 2016). It supports the notion that images can be used deliberately by children to represent their social worlds (Freeman & Mathison, 2008). What it also perhaps indicates is that it is likely to be helpful, where possible, for children to opt to choose particular means of representation if taking part in research – in many ways, what we are seeking is the best representation of ideation that we can find.

If children have produced an artefact, this can then be used to mediate communication in a way that would have been difficult without having it as a point of focus (Lipponen et al., 2016). Considering some of the symbols of communication that children may select to include in, for example, a photograph that they may have been able to manipulate, avoids the division that may arise from a lack of shared language that can culturally imbue meaning and hinder interaction.

One consideration that you may make is whether you are seeking to understand knowledge or develop knowledge through the processes that you are employing. Clark (2017) makes a distinction between knowledge extraction and knowledge creation, and emphasises that the latter forms part of participatory arts-based research. Certainly, where you may be encouraging children to reflect carefully on their own experiences, this process of reflection will help them learn about themselves as they take part in the research, and can be considered one of the benefits to children. However, you will also want to garner information about the meaning that children are applying in their reflections, so there will also be an element of knowledge extraction. One is not really effective without the other.

The way that this 'looks' in any particular instance will depend upon the nature of your research question – you may be asking children to reflect on their experiences of mathematics, but you may also want to understand what they know about this as a concept. For example, the children may make representations of their experiences that are related to particular feelings and meanings that the subject has for them, but they may only associate these with formally taught aspects of the subject. They may not necessarily recognise that adjusting the point of release of a ball in physical education determines its trajectory, and that this 'is' mathematics. Gaining an understanding of the children's perspectives here will therefore, as indicated above, be likely to involve a process of knowledge creation and knowledge extraction. The emphasis in creative approaches to research will be placed on the former, but do not be afraid to acknowledge the need for the latter also. The difference in knowledge extraction that is associated with creative approaches in research is that it is used to understand aspects of the implications of the subjective experiences of children, rather than judge them – it can even be used to then feed back into the circle of knowledge generation.

Therefore, although it is of value to see participants motivated by the methods that are chosen, it would perhaps be insufficient for this to be the sole rationalisation for a creative approach. The purpose of utilising an approach that demands enacted engagement by participants and researcher is ultimately to generate data that is meaningful and useful. The following section discusses the nature of data and its applicability to understanding meaning here.

Why use creative tools? Generation of rich data

Creative approaches are often justified in terms of arguments that suggest they create 'rich', nuanced data (Schulze, 2017). This is actually quite a challenging concept and it is not unusual to look at studies that purport to do this but that actually demonstrate a limited understanding of what is actually meant here. In the context being referred to in this instance, rich data reflects the complexities of experience represented. One way of conceptualising this is to consider three related dichotomies of significance that mean data are multifaceted (see Figure 2.5).

If we consider each of the features of rich data identified in Figure 2.5, creative approaches can produce data that is both tangible and abstract, having characteristics of both an object and an idea; is cognitive and sensory, both of

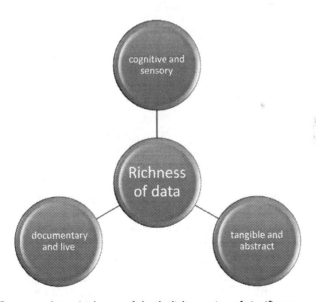

Figure 2.5 Conceptualising 'richness of data': dichotomies of significance

intellectual thought and emotional representation; and is simultaneously documentary and live, identifying detail of how something may have been experienced and, as a result, how this impacts on the child in the present. The considerations that need to be made as to how to actually generate this kind of quality data in relation to research tools are discussed in detail in Chapter 3, but your essential decision to employ any means of creative generation in research will be underpinned by a desire to generate this depth of data.

The production of artefacts in research can create what is a live document. Freeman and Mathison (2008) describe images, for example, as having a living quality. This emanates, in part, from the investment in their production, but what it can also do is give children an opportunity to develop their presentation and illustrate their thinking processes:

Scenario

I was working individually with Charlie as she was using the figures to represent playing with her friends at school in the tableau that she was creating. She'd created two 'hills' out of sand and put some of the characters on one and some on the other. We then chatted about who the figures represented, what they were doing, and why. As we were talking, she changed her mind about one of the figures and began to partially bury them in the sand ... 'there, that's better' she said, 'she can't get out to bother me now'.

In relation to some of the points made above illustrating the way in which children may spontaneously work across different media to make their point, I return to the idea that you may wish to experiment with giving children choices in their expression. This can present some challenges in generating viable data that can be analysed (see Chapter 4), but arguably means that children can choose a medium to suit them. Herein, you could create genuinely unique ways of exploring the complexity of experience. However, care also needs to be taken to ensure that endeavours to be different are appropriate and not just novel for their own sake (Nind & Vinha, 2016). Nevertheless, this individualisation can be a helpful means through which purpose is maintained.

Essentially, the reflection of the nature of knowledge and the relationship this has with using creative approaches, as advocated by researchers such as Mann and Warr (2017), forms the basis of arguing for the use of creative tools. The complexities of experiences, as reflected in their reconstruction for research purposes, form the basis of understanding individual subjectivities. In qualitative research it is the depth of understanding that underpins our interpretations – although often assumed to be creative in itself (Konecki, 2019), it is crucial that the selected approach adequately reflects the epistemological assumptions embedded in the essential research question.

If we think about how this relates to concepts of play and meaning, the way that children can manipulate research tools (such as those in, for example, modelling) creates a representation in recognisable form of what would have been an undifferentiated mass of material (Hammershoj, 2014). Hammershoj discusses expressions of imagination, but his conceptualisation can arguably also be applied to the concept of representation. Essentially, a child is invited to project their thoughts into the production of an artefact. This is, in itself, a dynamic phenomenon that can be reflective of the thought processes involved in considering experience, and can help in your selection of research tool.

There is an immediacy to creative approaches to research that mean they can carry in them a message for the observer (Freeman & Mathison, 2008; McCaffrey & Edwards, 2015), but reaching this apparent state has been carefully achieved through the mediation of thought and action in its production that is of value in establishing change (Stavropoulou, 2019). This means that we can argue that clear detail and depth of meaning is encompassed in these approaches. However, this can occur only when the research demonstrates clear integrity on behalf of you as a researcher.

Ethical considerations

The ethical considerations that you will need to make in relation to your research, as you consider taking a creative approach, essentially evolve around the purposes of your work and the way this is justified in establishing the ethical approvals discussed in Chapter 1. Kara (2015) suggests close alignment between creative thinking and ethical thinking, in that there is a transparency to such approaches that recognises influence and fallibility in research design.

One of the dangers of more 'traditional' forms of research, which are given ethical approval through procedural preferences that tend to favour scientific models of consent, are that they can lead to the exclusion of the very children whose perspectives we need to explore to improve practice that affects them (Arnott, Martinez-Lejarreta, Wall, Blaisdell, & Palaiologou, 2020; Brown, Spiro, & Quinton, 2020). Designing research that involves creative approaches can help reduce what could be described as the misalignment of formal research ethical approval designs that do not appear to facilitate, but rather obstruct, the inclusion of children as participants in research.

In practice, obtaining approval to work with children can also be compounded by a lack of specialisms in the expertise of those involved on ethical boards. Detailing the relationship between the research question, nature of inclusion, and the protective potential of creative approaches to research, can help with moving towards greater involvement of children and the expression of their voices. Therefore, with respect to your selection of research approach, clearly aligning discussions of this with your research topic and ensuring that the investment of your participants is purposeful and meaningful, both to you and your participants, ensures ethical practice as a priority, and also helps with obtaining approval in the first instance. This demands that the initial purposes of the research justify the approach, through establishing that this is the best or only way to create the data that is required to answer your specific research question (Graham, Powell, & Taylor, 2015).

In relation to this, as you progress to begin your research, children need to be facilitated in the control they have over how their data is generated, and this can be supported by including an element of choice in what they do and ensuring that there is an ongoing negotiated informed consent/assent process associated with this (Arnott et al., 2020). This obviously still needs to allow you to answer your research question, but giving children particular controls presents a democratic approach to your topic that is ethically viable. This choice can come from the selection of research tool (as discussed further in Chapter 3) and also from freedoms of manipulation of their artefact. This latter factor refers to the freedoms you allow in the way the children's data may evolve as they produce their artefact. In this way, this selection becomes an ethically underpinned process in itself.

Despite this, however, there may be situations where offering choice of approaches may not be appropriate for your data generation – for example, you may wish to use an approach where some children do not have particular advantages in artefact manipulation. Such a situation may arise from, as will be discussed in Chapter 3, different tools having different aspects of 'cool' and cultural accessibility. Therefore, there will be particular methods that are attractive to children. However, this could potentially disadvantage some if free choice is given. To explain: such an instance could be where, of your group, some have access to technology that enables them to manipulate digital images and others do not. Therefore, if a child chooses to use photographs to represent their experience because it is perceived as more culturally acceptable, but do not have either the skills or access to technology that allows them to manipulate the image if they wish to, then their photograph may not adequately incorporate representations that they would really like to convey. In such cases, a decision may be made (again, if appropriate to exploring the research question) to ask all participants to draw pictures.

Related to this is the possibility of using creative solutions to obtain consent and assent from participants to be involved in your study. Arnott et al. (2020) suggest that consent be negotiated with child participants through utilising creative approaches that outline information to participants. They explored tools, such as the use of animated video and narrative picture books, that explain research. Although the efficacy of these tools will vary, as will the way in which they are of value to use with particular groups of children, they do all form a basis on which opportunities for participants to ask questions and ascertain clarity of understanding can be structured (Arnott et al., 2020).

Overall, you need to be sure that your approach is one of focus and that you are not being creative 'for the sake of it'. There must be a strong rationale for taking these approaches (Mortari & Harcourt, 2012). Ask yourself what the purpose of your research is and how a creative approach is going to enable you to most effectively answer the questions that you are raising. Creativity is thought provoking and time consuming, and should only be engaged with if you are sure that you will be valuing the investment of all concerned.

Conclusion

This chapter has considered what we mean by creative approaches to research, how they serve to reflect research-evaluating experiences, and why they are particularly helpful with children. Attention has been given to the way in which creativity is something that determines research design and method selection, but that is also informed by your own thought processes as a creative researcher. Generating possibilities for divergent thinking that can disclose responses to your research topic that were unanticipated, creative research still retains a purposefulness in addressing appropriate research topics. This is dependent upon your discernment as a researcher in identifying relevance and meaning in data and processes.

As a result of this meaningful approach that incorporates concepts of process, creative methods can be enormously engaging for participants, particularly where they form part of children's cultural practices and, as such, are motivational. This engagement is not only due to the affinity participants may have for particular methods, but also the demands of the thought processes that children need to utilise in order to respond to the research task. The time required to anticipate and plan, execute and reflect, all assure a level of investment that draws children into the research topic in a meaningful way. Herein, the nature and level of engagement create a complexity of data that is 'rich' in its representation, consisting of both content and process that is relevant to the topic of investigation, and with an embodiment of the meaning the subject has for participants.

You should now have an understanding that, to be effective:

Creativity is both process and product – informing research design, tool selection and thinking throughout
Creative thinking is purposeful, relevant and meaningful – establishing and maintaining a relationship between research question, knowledge generation and understanding
Creative approaches require active engagement of participant and researcher – demanding slow thinking, investment and empathy
Creative approaches can generate rich data – simultaneously cognitive and sensory, tangible and abstract, documentary and live

Having established what we mean by the concept of creativity and the value of its place in research, the following chapter turns to consider the specific tools that we may employ with child participants, and the potential efficacy of these in practice. Attention is given to the absolute and relative value of different visual tools that can be utilised in creative research, and the dimensions of experience that can be conveyed through them. It also considers the control that different tools afford children's sense of collaboration, leading to a vibrant environment for data production.

References

Aldridge, J. (2012). The participation of vulnerable children in photographic research. *Visual Studies*, 27(1), 48–58. doi:10.1080/1472586X.2012.642957.

Arnott, L., Martinez-Lejarreta, L., Wall, K., Blaisdell, C., & Palaiologou, I. (2020). Reflecting on three creative approaches to informed consent with children under six. *British Educational Research Journal*, 46(4), 786–810. doi:10.1002/berj.3619.

Boden, M. (2010). *Creativity and Art: Three Roads to Surprise*. Oxford: Oxford University Press.

Brown, C., Spiro, J., & Quinton, S. (2020). The role of research ethics committees: friend or foe in educational research? An exploratory study. *British Educational Research Journal*, 46(4), 747–769. doi:10.1002/berj.3654.

Chesworth, L. (2016). A funds of knowledge approach to examining play interests: listening to children's and parents' perspectives. *International Journal of Early Years Education*, 24(3), 294–308. doi:10.1080/09669760.2016.1188370.

Clark, A. (2017). *Listening to Young Children: A Guide to Understanding and Using the Mosaic Approach*, Expanded 3rd ed. London: Jessica Kingsley Publishers.

Fautley, M., & Savage, J. (2007). *Creativity in Secondary Education*. Exeter: Learning Matters.

Freeman, M., & Mathison, S. (2008). *Researching Children's Experiences*. New York: Guilford Publications.

Graham, A., Powell, M. A., & Taylor, N. (2015). Ethical research involving children. *Family Matters*, (96), 23–28.

Hammershoj, L. G. (2014). Creativity in education as a question of cultivating sensuous forces. *Thinking Skills and Creativity*, 13, 168–182. doi:10.1016/j.tsc.2014.05.003.

Hanson, M. H. (2014). Converging paths: creativity research and educational practice. *Knowledge Quest*, 42(5), 8.

Jeffrey, B., Craft, A., & Leibling, M. (2001). *Creativity in Education*. London: Continuum.

Kara, H. (2015). *Creative Research Methods in the Social Sciences – A Practical Guide*. Bristol: Policy Press.

Konecki, K. T. (2019). Creative thinking in qualitative research and analysis. *Qualitative Sociology Review*, 15(3), 6–25. doi:10.18778/1733-8077.15.3.01.

Liamputtong, P. (2007). *Researching the Vulnerable: A Guide to Sensitive Research Methods*. London and Thousand Oaks, CA: SAGE.

Lipponen, L., Rajala, A., Hilppö, J., & Paananen, M. (2016). Exploring the foundations of visual methods used in research with children. *European Early Childhood Education Research Journal*, 24(6), 936–946. doi:10.1080/1350293X.2015.1062663.

Lomax, H. (2012). Contested voices? Methodological tensions in creative visual research with children. *International Journal of Social Research Methodology*, 15(2), 105–117. doi:10.1080/13645579.2012.649408.

Maksić, S. B., & Spasenović, V. Z. (2018). Educational science students' implicit theories of creativity. *Creativity Research Journal*, 30(3), 287–294. doi:10.1080/10400419.2018.1488200.

Mann, R., & Warr, D. (2017). Using metaphor and montage to analyse and synthesise diverse qualitative data: exploring the local worlds of 'early school leavers'. *International Journal of Social Research Methodology*, 20(6), 547–558. doi:10.1080/13645579.2016.1242316.

McCaffrey, T., & Edwards, J. (2015). Meeting art with art: arts-based methods enhance researcher reflexivity in research with mental health service users. *Journal of Music Therapy*, 52(4), 515–532. doi:10.1093/jmt/thv016.

Mortari, L., & Harcourt, D. (2012). 'Living' ethical dilemmas for researchers when researching with children. *International Journal of Early Years Education*, 20(3), 234–243. doi:10.1080/09669760.2012.715409.

Nind, M., & Vinha, H. (2016). Creative interactions with data: using visual and metaphorical devices in repeated focus groups. *Qualitative Research*, 16(1), 9.

Rose, G. (2016). *Visual Methodologies: An Introduction to Researching with Visual Materials*, 4th Ed. London: SAGE Publications.

Schulze, S. (2017). The value of two modes of graphic elicitation interviews to explore factors that impact on student learning in higher education. *Qualitative Sociology Review*, 13(2), 60–77.

Stavropoulou, N. (2019). Understanding the 'bigger picture': lessons learned from participatory visual arts-based research with individuals seeking asylum in the United Kingdom. *Crossings: Journal of Migration & Culture*, 10(1), 95–118. doi:10.1386/cjmc.10.1.95_1.

Zimmerman, J. (2015). *Hermeneutics – A Very Short Introduction*. Oxford: Oxford University Press.

Chapter 3

Selecting tools for creative research

> I think it's sort of cool that you get to use the camera.
>
> (Lottie, aged 12yrs)

This chapter will consider the nature of expression and how this might relate to individual children and groups as participants in research. The processes associated with the transference of cognitive concepts into visual forms as tools in research will be explored in light of generating meaning.

Chapter 2 discussed the complexities of creative approaches to research and endeavoured to establish that this is more than simply using creative tools in research. However, within this exploration, there is an essential assumption that tools utilised will be those of a creative/artistic nature. It is therefore helpful to consider the value of these tools as they may be used individually and/or offered as options for your children to select from. The emphasis here is on material data as a process of reification that is visually interpreted (Jewitt, Xambo, & Price, 2017; Lipponen, Rajala, Hilppö, & Paananen, 2016). Some principles, however, could be applied to other forms of expression, such as through music, as explored by McCaffrey and Edwards (2015).

Key discussion points will include:

- Types of visual expression:
    a   Drawings – freehand, mapping/diagrammatic tools, graphic-elicitation
    b   Photographs – photo-elicitation, photo-voice, video
    c   Collage and 3-D representations
    d   Diaries and other written forms of expression
- Ethical considerations

On a most basic level, visual expression requires thoughtful engagement as it demands 'thinking time' (Angell & Angell, 2013). It also, arguably, aligns to the way in which we formulate thought, as we will generally visualise ideas before we express them. The evolution of an environment in which creative tools are used has been seen as a positive shift in the social sciences (Jewitt et al., 2017) and is positioned as making a key contribution to new ways of questioning (Chesworth, 2016). Justifications can be very comprehensive with their participatory and practical nature supporting the inclusion of children (Lipponen et al., 2016). The cognitive preparation involved, one of thoughtful reflection, considered representation and improved personal understanding (Freeman & Mathison, 2008; Mannay, Staples, & Edwards, 2017), is considered to benefit both the research process and participants themselves. As recollections of experiences will not always follow an ordered pattern, the use of arts-based tools enables children to present experience in non-linear ways (Culshaw, 2019) and provides an expanded 'toolbox' of methodological possibilities (Mann & Warr, 2017). Many visual methods have emanated from use in therapy and, although often overlooked, it is possible for similarities to be drawn between the two in the sense that children's engagement can support reflection and help them understand their own experiences (Mannay et al., 2017).

Types of visual expression

This section will give an overview of different types of visual expression that you may decide to use with children in a school environment. I focus here on the value of each and why they may be seen as an effective means of data generation in relation to understanding children's perspectives. Considerations regarding how their usefulness is ensured, in terms of being viable data, is discussed in Chapter 4, but here I will attend to the need to ascertain your own understanding of what the visual image/text/artefact is representing, which will be crucial in ensuring that you can adequately analyse the data. If we are to share experiences, they require a form of materialisation (Lipponen et al., 2016).

It has been suggested that we live in an ocularcentric culture (Culshaw, 2019) and that the world is dominated by visual imagery (Ledin & Machin, 2018). This identifies that the visual representation of meaning permeates our social world and, by implication, that this is an accessible form of communication within modern society for most individuals. Such an environment has been particularly facilitated by advances in technology and the everyday accessibility of means to both produce and consume images (Chesworth, 2016; Ledin & Machin, 2018). Therefore, interpreting imagery for different purposes is something that most of us are accustomed to doing. Arguably, many of us are also used to producing images for particular purposes; to provoke a specific response. As discussed in Chapter 2, this can be very significant for young people in particular. So, the question here is regarding what ways visual representation of experience might enable participants in research to express their experience in a meaningful way.

As identified above, visual methods of research with children are justified on the basis that they are both participatory and practical (Lipponen et al., 2016). The earliest, and arguably most frequently used means of using visual methods with children has focused on drawings (Kara, 2015).

Using drawings in research with children

Drawings are frequently considered an appropriate tool for conducting research with children, as they are seen to be embedded in cultural practices and enjoyable artefacts to create (Carless & Lam, 2014; Schulze, 2017). Their history in art therapy also means they have been associated with understanding children for some time (Freeman & Mathison, 2008). Creating a drawing is a deeply subjective action and a process that children are used to in terms of acting as a symbolic resource (Freeman & Mathison, 2008); as such, it can be reflective of the individualised experiences of the individual producing it. Further, on a practical level, using drawings requires few resources (Schulze, 2017) and is a very straightforward tool to employ within school settings.

As they are considered to form part of everyday practices in teaching, schools are frequently considered an appropriate location within which to work with participants on drawings. It may also be the case that drawings are selected as a tool for research purely *because* the research is being conducted in a school (particularly in the earlier years of education). Additionally, researchers may ask the teachers themselves to oversee children completing drawings as a class activity for research, making this approach attractive purely on the basis of efficiency (Freeman & Mathison, 2008). Either way, for pragmatic reasons, there is a sense of convenience and 'good fit' here. Indeed, this is logical.

However, conveniently producing class drawings en masse does have its drawbacks – for example, children can see each other's drawings, which can influence what they do, particularly as they can be self-conscious about what they have selected to draw and concerned it will be judged by peers. Do not be surprised if you have a whole series of drawings that look really similar to those of children's friends. This may not necessarily be problematic if you are using this tool in conjunction with others, but it will limit what conclusions you can infer about the drawing itself or its content. More detailed consideration as to how you might ensure drawings have the complex value that you are aiming for is included in Chapter 4, but suffice to note here that some of the arguments 'for' using drawing in research can be mitigated by the environment, and other contextual issues if not managed well. It is particularly difficult to avoid the sense that children perceive themselves as 'good', or not, at drawing:

> I liked that we used drawings cos I like drawing and that's what I'm good at.
> (Trina, aged 9yrs)

> I sort of thought the drawing bit was ok but I'm sort of not good at drawing and other people are better than me so it's not a good thing for that.
> (Rosie, aged 9yrs)

The argument that engaging in drawing as an activity is a 'natural' or culturally embedded activity is, however, simplistic in its assumptions. This is not to say it is not an appropriate method, but clear consideration needs to be given to the way in which it is presented to children, and the choice that the child has not to engage and/or select an alternative means of representation. Generally, things to look out for that could impact on the response you are seeking may be:

- Children think they are going to be judged on their artistic competencies
- If completed in a class context, children may copy one another
- Children may draw only those things that they believe are culturally desirable

It is imperative that the artistic quality of the artefact produced by children is not a feature of expectations and that you, as a researcher, do not comment on this (either positively or negatively). You can express approval to your participant by making comments about how interesting what they are doing/have achieved is, but should not make a value judgement about detail or perspective, for example. What is important is the intention behind what the child is seeking to represent.

Drawing, words and relating the two

Drawing as representation may require verification and, at times, children will find ways of doing this of their own volition. As I indicated in the introduction to this book, my interest in using drawings in research with children arose from their having used them instinctively in diaries that they were keeping about their experiences of physical education. Following this, my interest in using drawings grew; when I did this, however, as identified in Chapter 2, I found that children would instinctively add words that they felt explained the drawing (even if they knew they would be given an opportunity to explain their drawings at a later point). They would also label individuals in the pictures (even where they had been asked not to). This 'accidental' discovery bears some resemblance to the more deliberately designed 'draw and write' technique developed by Werron, wherein children respond to a topic by drawing a picture and writing a short piece associated with it before discussing perspective (Kara, 2015). Largely used to explore questions of health and to assess an associated educational intervention, this has been seen as a comprehensive approach to understanding children's perspectives.

This technique has focused on children of primary school age, however, the use of words in conjunction with drawings is also effective with secondary school children, and there appears to be a kind of security that young people have in adding key terms that they feel explain their pictures. What this also enables them to do is explain their use of metaphor where they employ this in their images.

In some language-based research, the use of particular terminology that was used as metaphor to communicate meaning was identified as specific to children (Fletcher, 2013). In drawings, metaphor is also employed by children to convey

Figure 3.1 Drama as 'cool' (Kelly, aged 14yrs)

intentions. Figure 3.1 not only uses words but also the metaphor of the wind to represent 'coolness', which is itself a linguistic metaphor for something that is desirable in youth culture. Where there is free choice, this kind of technique tends to be used more by young people than younger children, as the latter will be more literal in their approach. This also highlights the need to ensure that participants have the opportunity to explain their drawings in order to create viable data and ensure accurate representation.

You may additionally find that some young people assume drawing to be a childish activity, and care in presenting the idea with respect to making it age-appropriate is needed. As Milly said in her evaluation of drawing as an approach:

> The only thing I'd say is it's a bit like for little kids.
>
> (Milly, aged 13yrs)

For children in secondary school, if I have used drawings as a tool, I have asked young people to complete them in their own time, and therefore away from the 'gaze' of others. In one instance, this meant that children produced a computer-generated image, which proved much more effective in terms of its cultural accessibility. This was something I had not anticipated but which was helpful when thinking about what is most appropriate for children.

A further consideration to make is of how children are made aware of the potential 'audience' that will be interpreting their drawing. In most instances, this will probably be you alone as the researcher, and whoever may ultimately read your work. If the class or subject teacher is also likely to see the pictures, this needs to be made clear to the children. Such factors also need to be acknowledged when you write up your research, as anticipated audiences may affect the drawings that children produce (Burkitt, Watling, & Message, 2019).

Freehand drawing is therefore a highly malleable form of communication. However, particularly in light of some concerns with the medium, other forms of drawing, such as mapping, can also be a useful research tool.

Drawing maps and other diagrammatic tools

There are a number of mapping techniques that can be used in research (Bridger, 2013). For example, if you are working with children on their use of spaces, you could very specifically ask them to map this out. This could help identify where they go and their activities in these places (Bridger, 2013; Freeman & Mathison, 2008; Kara, 2015).

This is clearly using drawing as an adjunct tool, i.e. one whose purpose is really only to facilitate later discussion. The expression in this instance will come at a later point in the research. However, the approach still offers a degree of control and decision making with the child, and therefore provides a visual reference and way of mitigating against power differentials of researcher/ participant and adult/child, as will be discussed in Chapter 5.

If considering social relationships, it is also possible to give a pre-drawn diagram for children to write in – concentric circles can provide a framework for expressing closeness (Kara, 2015), as in Figure 3.2.

Figure 3.2 is a very simple example of a social map that can be used with children in school. Participants could write names or draw pictures of those who affect their experiences, which can then form the basis for discussion. This also raises the potential that drawings not produced by children themselves can be used in creative approaches to research, and most often employed where a graphic elicitation technique is used.

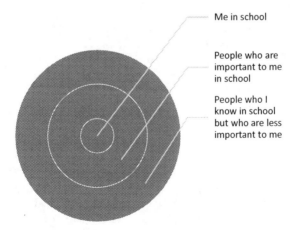

Figure 3.2 Simple social mapping

Graphic elicitation

Therefore, further to children manipulating different types of drawing, graphic representations can be used as stimuli to discuss particular topics with them. Whether produced entirely by children themselves or framed through mapping or other means as described above, graphic elicitation is the use of diagrams as stimuli in research, and can be particularly useful if exploring complex relationships (Bridger, 2013) or dealing with what may be sensitive issues (Schulze, 2017). Again, this is a way of highlighting conceptions that may not have been anticipated.

Further forms of drawing, such as creating time maps, can also be used, for example where it may be important to consider sequences of events for children. This is also considered to be a type of drawing that can be used for elicitation purposes in research (Schulze, 2017).

Whilst many forms of graphics in this type of research are illustrations, photographs can also be used for such purposes through employing photo-elicitation techniques (Bridger, 2013) and can be particularly useful, for example, in working with children who have additional learning needs. However, photographs taken by children themselves can create the possibility of using photo-voice techniques, which may be more meaningful in the research process.

The use of photographs: photo-elicitation

Photo-elicitation techniques involve the use of images that are taken by the researcher and used to frame an interview (Harper, 2012). Rose (2016) suggests that photo-elicitation techniques can be particularly useful in foregrounding aspects of 'everyday' experiences. If a researcher were, for example, to follow a class through a week, taking photographs of each day, interviews with children could then be built around these photographs to construct a representation of what they experience in daily school life. This can centralise what normally remains implicit as important, particularly as this affects children so significantly. Harper (2012) has identified that photo-elicitation can be a way for participants to respond to images, by generating their own narrative that claims an experience as their own. This way, an understanding of the children's perspectives is generated and value is acknowledged in a way that has previously been absorbed by what appears as the ordinariness of life. However, there has been a lack of use of this approach in educational research (Torre & Murphy, 2015).

When conducting research in school, there are sometimes instances where access to particular contexts for you as a researcher is not feasible, as you may impact on the actions that you want to come to understand. I have found that in such an instance, it can be helpful to enrol the support of staff who may be in a better position to generate the images. In one instance I asked a staff member to take photographs so that I could understand what children were doing and then used the images to speak to them about it. This was in a piece of research concerning children taking on playground leadership roles. In order to interpret the experiences, the teaching assistant, who had overall responsibility for the children involved, took photographs to be used in later discussions with them.

This helped both me, in terms of seeing what happened, and also the participants, in acting as triggers for discussion. When the photographs were then used to talk to the children, they served to help support recollections. We can see an example of this in the group interview below:

CHLOE: Oh look at that one – look at that one – can you remember that?
HARRIET: Yeah yeah! It was when Georgie tried to be the leader too and she wanted to tell everyone what to do when actually she was s'posed to just be playing the game.
ELISE: Yeah – and the little people hated it and we had to help her to know that she wasn't s'posed to be doing that ....

So, I was able to see some of the activities that the girls had engaged in and then, as can be seen from the above speech, one of the images that the girls selected to focus on triggered a particular memory and, in doing so, enabled them to reconstruct that specific experience.

Using photographs can also be an effective elicitation technique to support children's contribution when other forms of participation could be more difficult for them:

> **Scenario**
>
> *I was completing research with a class of children aged 9 and 10yrs. One child, Jake, worked with a teaching assistant and was not present when we completed drawings. Concerned that he would perhaps have some difficulty in understanding the research task to complete the drawing independently, Jake joined the research at the interview stage. At that point, the researcher used images created by the teaching assistant, based on the knowledge that she had of Jake's family, to help him explain what he liked about being physically active within and outside of school – it really helped with having a conversation and ensuring his perspectives were included in the research.*

It could also be helpful for you to consider, as Luttrell (2010) did, generating the opportunity for children to freely look at one another's photographs – peer group audiencing – identifying what they notice in the images and asking questions of the photographer. Such dialoguing between children can create a new sense of meaning and again highlight points that may not emerge from conversations you may hold as a researcher. This approach rather links ideas of photo-elicitation and photo-voice, as they involve pictures generated by the children but have the discussion led by others. The value of this is that a new interrogative voice is gained to support interpretation.

Photo-voice

Further developing the idea of using photographs in research with children is the concept of photo-voice. Although photo-elicitation and photo-voice are sometimes confused, they do each have differences and purposes that emanate from their respective research heritages (Barriage & Hicks, 2020). According to Rose (2016), photo-voice tends to involve projects where images are being produced in accordance with a particular theme, defined by a research question, and are always generated by participants. Each of these approaches, however, can be a useful tool in exploring more sensitive issues (Kara, 2015) and working with vulnerable children (Aldridge, 2012). Photo-voice, however, carries with it a 'subtext of empowerment' (Harper, 2012), and can therefore be seen as more meaningful in terms of research processes. Within this, it also draws a sense of creativity from the participant, and is therefore of particular value when working with children.

Thinking about the context of using photo-voice with children, we now see a distinct difference in the way photographs form part of everyday society (Ledin & Machin, 2018). Previously used within classrooms as records or decoration rather than a sense-making tool (Lodge, 2009), this has changed significantly and impacted on how photographs can be used in research with children. Historically, photographs have been seen as a form of reductive realism (Spencer, 2011) in order to present 'factual' evidence as documentation. However, as their use has developed, they have been employed not only in this way but also symbolically, and, as they become increasingly malleable, utilised in research to convey experience. This potential for manipulation is reflective of photograph use in research as it has progressed from being a means to transpose realistic form to becoming a meaningful expression of emotion (Freeman & Mathison, 2008; Rissanen, 2020).

Therefore, photographs do not necessarily represent any kind of truth of participant's experience but can share perspectives through visual representation (Aldridge, 2012). Like drawings, photo-voice has been identified as a way of handing control to children (Swartz, 2011). It is a concept wherein individuals can use photographs to express their experiences and can be a helpful, indeed powerful, tool when working with children as a marginalised group (Barriage & Hicks, 2020; Freeman & Mathison, 2008; Luttrell, 2010).

As such, photographs have been identified as having the potential to play a key role in communicating children's experiences and understanding what is significant to them (Lipponen et al., 2016). They also generate possibilities for new narratives about familiar topics (Luttrell, 2010). For example, Sanderud (2020) found that children took photographs of images that had not directly been encouraged or anticipated, creating new possibilities regarding the way the researcher had been thinking.

One question to be considered, when exploring the idea of using photographs, is that of whether you wish to use single snapshots or a series of images. This will depend on your research question and what is most appropriate to address your aims. Individual photographs can have a singularity through which children might summarise their experience; multiple photographs can illustrate different aspects of experience or experience over time, as in the work of Aldridge (2012). A series of images potentially takes more of a storied form of sharing through which children can explore not only key points, as illustrated in the images, but the transition between phases of experience. Linked to the idea that photographs can give the researcher 'first-hand' experience of a topic (Sanderud, 2020), this can be a useful inroad to understand perspectives directly through the eyes of children.

In wider visual culture, photographs may be contextualised in that they have a background, which visually and conceptually (potentially) frames the subject, or they may be decontextualized, wherein a plain background is used (Ledin & Machin, 2018). Children can find ways of creating these kinds of impression within their digital images (e.g. through removing or blurring backgrounds) and can make clear where the focus of the meaning needs to be (see Figure 3.3).

In Figure 3.3, Molly identifies herself as holding up her hand, not just physically as she takes on a leadership role in the context she is representing here, but also figuratively in the sense of learning to volunteer, to take on the concept of holding your hand 'up' rather than 'out'. This photograph raises the possibility of considering when photographs should be taken and for what purpose. In this particular instance, the image was selected retrospectively as a representation from a selection taken for other purposes. The background was then blurred to create a focal point to use for the research project. The potential to alter and enhance images in such ways means that children can have far more control over their final product than has previously been the case in research. This, therefore, also means that a more accurate representation of intention can be made.

Figure 3.3 Molly's representation of her leadership programme (aged 14yrs)

The practicalities of using photographs

Using photography with children presents particular practical considerations. The feasibility of using cameras in schools in research has previously been facilitated by the emergence of disposable cameras. This takes away some of the earlier concerns associated with children utilising expensive equipment unsupervised. In work with children in school I have given small groups a camera to share and then utilised the pictures, once developed, at a later date to talk through their selection. However, with a growth in digital technology, decrease in price and desire to manipulate images, it has become more appropriate and effective to use low priced digital cameras with children. Dependent upon the context that you are working in, it may also be reasonable for young people to use their smartphones to take images, as this forms a more culturally integrated approach to your research (Barriage & Hicks, 2020). This also facilitates the practicalities of sharing the images once they have been created. Any digital approach means children can also check the appearance of an image to ensure it is as they would wish it to be, and has even been described as an 'effortless tool' through which children express themselves (Rissanen, 2020). It is important to remember, as well, that the way in which you ask children to approach the research can impact on how participants engage and how they are seen by others in this engagement. Where you place value will draw children's attention and help focus their photography. Alternatively, as in the example above, images that have been created during particular experiences can be selected to represent that experience as a whole.

Where cameras do not directly form part of the culture of an environment you are investigating, some authors have identified the novelty of using them as taking participants attention over and above the purposes of the research, at least in initial stages (Lipponen et al., 2016). This is not necessarily problematic, as long as you bear this in mind when you analyse your data. Indeed, it may ultimately create greater engagement with what you are doing as it can give status to participants and add value to the process from the perspective of the children:

> I think it's sort of cool that you get to use the camera.
>
> (Lottie, aged 12yrs)

Part of this response will depend on how you present the research to children. In her research, Luttrell (2010) elected to tell children that using cameras was a big responsibility in terms of their material value. This can be of benefit but can also result in some children having a reluctance to use them, as they become afraid of damaging them. There may also be instances where parents become involved at home if the cameras are taken out of school, to keep the cameras safe, which may not be appropriate for what you are hoping to achieve with your participants. The most important thing is to make your expectations clear and ensure that this facilitates the integrity of the research.

Considering the responses that children have to drawing in research, there is a similar need to ensure that children are given the opportunity to add words to their images to explain and expand on what they represent. This creates a kind of dual purpose for photographs and text, meaning it operates on the level of the image itself and also the explanation of its meaning/expansion of the experience(s) associated with it (Freeman & Mathison, 2008). It may therefore be helpful for children, where age appropriate, to add a caption to their pictures – this can be used as data in itself or can give an additional dimension to the information you have prior to talking to children, and can support your preparation.

What you may also find is that, as with drawings, older children will use metaphor (in my experience, from around the age of 12yrs) in their photographs. Luttrell (2010) suggests that photographs in themselves serve as a metaphor for experience – it is also possible that children use deliberate selection of metaphor to convey their thoughts (see Figure 3.4).

In Figure 3.4, Jessie is using metaphor to represent the hierarchical order that they perceive to exist in relationships between children in school. This is illustrative of the value in taking an approach where you could specifically ask children to cast their experience in a single photograph that acts as a metaphor for this (Fletcher, 2013). It also indicates the need to ensure you talk to children about their images, as photographs are rarely sufficient in themselves as research data (Drew & Guillemin, 2014).

Many children, though, focus on using photographs as documentary, as they feel secure in doing so:

> It's good because photos give evidence – strong evidence.
> (Jake, aged 14yrs)

Figure 3.4 Hierarchies in school (Jessie, aged 14yrs)

How children respond to taking photographs, however, does potentially involve a degree of frustration:

> It's sort of difficult because sometimes what you want to take a photo of just isn't there.
>
> (Helen, aged 15yrs)

Or, in a further instance:

> It's sometimes a bit stupid because if you're doing the thing, you can't be taking a photo of it.
>
> (Caleb, aged 14yrs)

Therefore, it may be worth ensuring that, even in instances where you want the choice of approach to photography to remain free, you discuss possibilities for representation with your participants.

One of the advantages of using cameras in research is that it can create the opportunity for the researcher to inhabit spaces that would not otherwise have been accessible to them (Aldridge, 2012). This has implications, not only in the sense that you may not have established a particular perspective, but also in terms of what physical space you could access. As a result, it also raises the question of children's mobility around school and which areas they can access in order to take a photograph. Although an advantage is seen in children's ability to select what they capture and represent from their surroundings (Sanderud, 2020), Vaswani (2018) identified that children may be restricted in what they can photograph by their limited ability to access particular places. Vaswani was considering the position of young migrants and her research has its own set of circumstances in a larger scale, but considering the points that she raised, we can apply this principle to consider children in school.

Thinking about the geographical environment, children's movement can be limited by a range of factors, which may include considerations such as age (certain year groups being restricted to particular buildings/open space); status (where schools have privileged roles that give some children the ability to enter certain areas that others are not permitted to do so); time of day (children can go to certain places before or after school hours but not during); and so on. There are also informal rules of engagement that children have about where they 'can and cannot' go. Although not necessarily immutable, these unwritten expectations regarding student relationships may well be outside of your understanding as a researcher. This could therefore dictate what pictures children are able to take, and when, and is something you need to make a conscious effort to understand when setting out your research.

Considering what may be comfortable for young people to respond to, you could also consider the format through which their photographs are shared. Photosharing on a website, or using social media platforms or specific 'apps', may be appropriate media to employ in some circumstances (Barriage & Hicks, 2020). However, this carries with it its own set of circumstances that need consideration, particularly with reference to ethical considerations (Poynter, 2010).

Some of the concerns associated with the use of photographs are linked to the process of analysis, which some authors have acknowledged may be determined by the perspectives of the researcher as 'reader' of the images (Sanderud, 2020). This is potentially because, although children are selecting images based on their own subjective interpretation, that image then appears as an 'object' that can be interpreted by someone else. As with drawings, it is therefore crucial that you ensure you have had some kind of explanation of the image(s) from your participants to confirm their intentions, as discussed in Chapter 4.

Use of video

It is also possible to utilise video in visual research as a means of facilitating voice (Meager, 2017), however, doing this in a school setting can be hugely problematic if being used for documentary purposes, e.g. to record day-to-day 'life' of participants, as there would be a lack of control over who was included in the video. The reality is, too, that ethical obstacles will often mean it is not really feasible to use this. It also has huge implications for data analysis, which proves highly complex (Kara, 2015), and there are further questions regarding how the video is interpreted by the researcher, with concerns that there is a tendency to present researcher rather than participant view (Meager, 2017).

Some researchers have used video in the fashion of photo-elicitation interviews, e.g. Chesworth's (2016) work on play in which video of children's free interactions was used to elicit parent responses. This was, however, clearly with children and adults who were responsible for them, and therefore circumvents the ethical minefield that would exist in working for different purposes without this element to the research.

Perhaps the most likely way in which you may be able to work with video in research in school is through the production of film designed as a creative artefact to represent experience. Through this, a creative product (the content of which is limited and controllable in the same way that photographs are) may be used as data. To explore this further, the National Centre for Research Methods has documented ways in which video can be used for research (Jewitt et al., 2017).

This is a way of working with children to generate 'film', rather than just being a video of a particular subject. Here, there is a specific design that is intended to convey specific messages – planning a theme of particular importance that is then plotted to share experiences. Essentially this provides the opportunity for children to document their school experiences with the potential to challenge dominant conceptualisations (Meager, 2017). This is an approach that requires working with children over a period of time, and possibly is best formed linking with curriculum study or extra-curricular clubs. A storyboard can be created to plan out the video, identifying key points of importance. Therefore, relationships with staff and students would be essential to ensuring appropriate procedures and protocols are in place (Pithouse-Morgan, Van Laren, Singh, & Mudaly, 2013). The final product could, however, be well controlled by children and be valuable in understanding particular issues.

Collage and 3-D representations of meaning

Another creative way through which children may represent their experiences is through collage, wherein a range of images or objects may be organised in a 'picture' and used to convey meaning. This can create a montage of individual experiences that represents the whole.

Collage can be an effective visual method for children, removing the need to draw and involve artistry (Roberts & Woods, 2018). This approach slows down the meaning-making process and allows children to rearrange elements of their image as they think through their experience (Culshaw, 2019; Roberts & Woods, 2018). This latter point also creates possibilities to generate a new narrative as children reconsider what they are doing, and it may be appropriate to talk to children about their thought processes as they engage in them. Collage also adds the potential for children to use different textures to convey meaning.

Furthermore, there is also the possibility to use elements of collage to create 3-D representations. In Figure 3.5, Joseph has created different representations of himself in a 'You-Cube'.

This concept of texture touches on the idea of the implications that creating a 3-D representation can have. Using clay-like material, such as play doh or plasticine, or even building bricks, as with collaging creates the possibility for children to reform what they are doing and can give additional information that may not have come across in 2-D imaging. In Figure 3.6, Tom has created a picture of his head of 'Me at school', and in Figure 3.7, Jeremy has done the same.

In Figure 3.7, Jeremy identifies his lack of confidence in school and how he likes to try to 'keep out of the way' of teachers and other children. He represents how he reduces his visibility by creating as flat an image as possible using the medium provided, creating an immediate illustration of the way he perceives himself differently to other children.

This approach can be particularly useful with younger children, although it is also worthwhile to check with the class teachers what their likely capabilities are. Children can find plasticine difficult to manipulate, while more ambitious children can find it frustrating if trying to add detail with playdoh as, if trying to link pieces, it often does not 'stick'. As regards to these materials, each of these can be reused so it is economically and environmentally efficient (just remember to take a photograph of what is produced in case you need to revisit some of the data). However, using coloured air drying clay solves some of the issues of manipulation and can mean the children can take their finished model

Figure 3.5 Joseph's representation of himself in a 'You-Cube' (aged 7yrs)

home with them. This way they can feel they have gained more from their efforts, may receive praise at home because of this, and parents/guardians can see what they have done as part of the research. Again, though, it is of value to take a picture of what has been produced for later use. These pictures can also be used when you write up your research to illustrate key points.

These approaches arguably have a more embodied nature to them and, similar to other embodied forms of expression, may actually expand creative capacity (Giguere, 2011). Creating 3-D artefacts means that children may develop a consciousness of themselves in relation to your research topic, as they project emotion as a viewable object (Mannay et al., 2017). Mannay et al. (2017) discuss the way in which children might create a sandbox scene that is representative of their s.bjective experience but observable by an audience as an object. Here, children use figures in sand to create a 'picture' that expresses thoughts and feelings symbolically. Considering the variations in dimension

46 Selecting tools for creative research

Figure 3.6 'Me at school' (Tom, aged 6yrs)

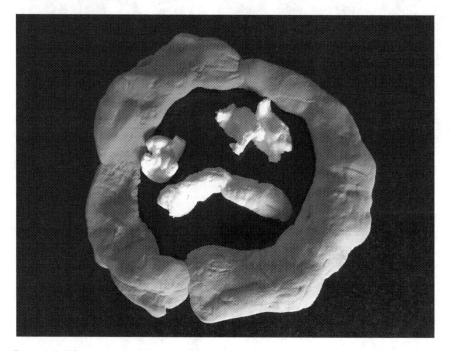

Figure 3.7 'Me at school' (Jeremy, aged 5yrs)

Selecting tools for creative research   47

Figure 3.8 Charlie's sandbox of groups of children in her class

that were, for example, expressed in the modelling of Figures 3.6 and 3.7, sandboxing creates the possibility of 'burying' items, as discussed in Chapter 2. This means that children can fully or partially obscure objects as well as show them in particular formations (see Figure 3.8).

All of the examples above attend to the concept of creativity in research and potentially avoid a dependence upon language that children can sometimes find difficult. However, many of these approaches are enhanced by language (as will be discussed in Chapter 4), and written texts can provide similar opportunities for creativity as pure visual imagery. This next section considers, in particular, the use of diaries and other forms of communication for children in creative research, and the values these have.

Written research data and the use of diaries with children

Many authors identify a range of written tools as forming valuable creative data. The use of written forms in research have also been identified as effective tools in research – creating prose responses and poems can be very effective in responding to research questions (Freeman & Mathison, 2008; Kara, 2015). These will effectively create representative outputs that can be further explored with children. Related to this concept of written approaches to research with children is that of the use of vignettes. In most instances, pre-prepared vignettes are used with children to represent particular concepts (Burkitt, Watling, & Cocks,

2019; Burkitt, Watling, & Message, 2019). Burkitt has used these when exploring children's conceptualisations of emotion pairs (e.g. 'happy' and 'sad'), but they can also be useful if used to present examples of experiences of children that can then be responded to by your participants. Children themselves could also create factual vignettes to convey their own experiences of particular situations.

Creative written approaches to research can also involve solicited diaries/journals of participants (Kara, 2015). These can be particularly useful if you are seeking to generate a documented account of children's experiences. These can also be more useful for children who would feel less able to produce an arts-based representation or who feel they can be more precise in their control over what they are producing. It has the value of similar characteristics of image-creating tools in that it is likely to require a degree of thought and planning (Freeman & Mathison, 2008). As identified in Chapter 2, they can have the advantage of perceiving that such methods require investment from the researcher. They also provide the opportunity for children to have a direct, private conversation with you. Sarah wrote in her 'PE diary':

> Then the girls went and as usually Claire and Susan won it's just not fair they went last time. usually Nathalie Jones would win but she hurt her neck so she couldn't do it but if she did do it she would win because she is a bof (don't tell her I told you that) In the end I ended up with some other people putting away the mats LIFE'S UNFAIR (sic).
>
> (Sarah, aged 12yrs, diary entry)

What this kind of diary entry can do also is indicate the level of trust that children have in you as a researcher, and the knowledge that you will keep a confidence. This can include when talking about other individuals, most notably teachers, that they would perhaps not do in other contexts:

> Mr Harrison really … doesn't know about not being good.
>
> (Andrew, aged 13yrs, diary entry)

Although not visual in the sense that some of the earlier tools discussed here are, there is added potential for this to be incorporated, as children will tend to manipulate their writing, adding in pictures and notes to you directly as the researcher.

There can also be a sense that, if used as a tool in isolation from others, children feel they have control over what is going to be derived from their diary:

> I liked the diary because you can say exactly what you want – you can explain it for the person that's not there.
>
> (Layla, aged 12yrs)

Diaries can also circumvent inaccurate recall (Kara, 2015). They can therefore be used as a tool in themselves, and also as a reflective tool representing documented events for later discussion.

A further option that may be helpful when working with children in their diaries is to suggest that they may choose to write in the first or third person. The latter can give a sense of an externalised perspective that can sometimes help children when speaking about themselves. However, it is also notable that children may change their orientation if the incident being conveyed is more emotional for them. In the extract below, Ellie had been maintaining a diary written in the third person – here she begins the entry maintaining this perspective for the first part of the opening sentence, however, she then abruptly switches to speaking in the first person:

> Ellie played netball and I made a mistake, so my group had to run round the court again they were not happy Chappies, I am not their friend know (sic).
> (Ellie, aged 12yrs, diary entry)

In talking to Ellie about the incident it was clearly one that had affected her more widely in school, beyond the PE lesson that she was referring to and, as indicated by the change of presentation, the diary entry was much more personal than her other entries had been. Therefore, when using diaries, you will have not only the information as portrayed in the content of what children write, but also how they present it. With careful consideration, this will alert you to some of the meanings that children carry in what they describe.

One thing to be cautious of with diaries is the way in which maintaining them may be considered similar to homework, and as such may impact on children's engagement and/or mean that parents are tempted to influence outcomes (Freeman & Mathison, 2008). Therefore, for young people in particular, using digital messaging may also be an appropriate alternative to writing diaries that can still be a means of understanding ongoing thoughts from children on what they are experiencing. Young people may be more comfortable with blogging or micro-blogging (e.g. Twitter) than other forms of generating data (Poynter, 2010). This can form a more instinctive means of writing for young people as it is frequently embedded into their culture (Freeman & Mathison, 2008). This would also be a way of combining written forms and imagery, following patterns of preparing material that young people may use with social media. It is important that you are familiar with the type of media that children engage in and in what way. This will include having an awareness of things such as age restrictions and permissions, but also, crucially, in what the children themselves consider to be appropriate means of communication.

As identified earlier in this text, what is important is the purpose and directions that frame the tool's use (Freeman & Mathison, 2008). It is also of value to consider how the artistic representations are shared with you. For example, a poem will have a different meaning if presented on paper as compared to being read to you as an audience. Incorporating a 'performance' element to what you are doing extends the potential for personalised representation if children have a preference for this. It can also create possibilities to extend consideration as to intended audiences and how these may focus a child's message.

Keeping a diary (or other 'real time' noting) has a specific focus on children recording experience in a way that is aligned with when it is occurring. As such, they have the potential to be utilised in three ways. First, simply in themselves, with you as a researcher interpreting the narrative that the children have presented without further detail from them. This could include reference to observation of the experiences children are describing, e.g. if they are conveying what has happened in their lessons, you may have had the opportunity to observe these lessons to compare what appeared to be happening 'objectively' to what was being experienced subjectively. Second, you could also speak to the children as they have made their entries in an ongoing process, either on a regular basis or as they maintain their records. Finally, they may be used once a particular episode of teaching has been completed. These changes affect the temporal location of the experience you may be seeking to understand and, as a result, will give a different perspective. A combination of these can also be utilised – this is effective in establishing a more complex picture of experiences as it is possible to see how some elements of experience are important at a particular time but do not have a long-lasting impact, while others have a more profound effect on the child.

Ethical considerations

In terms of ethical considerations relating to the production of artefacts in research, there is a particular concern now regarding child safeguarding with respect to identifying themselves and others in the process. Ordinarily such points are considered most pertinent where participants are taking photographs of themselves and other people. This will apply in terms of what is appropriate with reference to the ethical expectations of the school and your institution, and your own experience in relation to these.

Anecdotally, it is increasingly difficult to obtain ethical approval for children to take photographs around school, but it may be possible for you to achieve this. As discussed in Chapter 2, this will very much depend on the strength of rationalisation that you can present to justify the need for your particular approach in relation to your research question (Mortari & Harcourt, 2012). Justification here can be supported through assurances that work using the tools of photography of some kind will be anonymised through the use of techniques such as pixelation, block-out bars, blurring or perhaps cropping images to remove identifying features (Allen, 2015).

It is also important, however, to be mindful that these concerns are not limited to photography. It is not unusual for children to name individuals in drawings, for example, even where they have been asked not to. These instances clearly occur after ethical approval has been obtained and have implications for the way in which you use your data, rather than prepare to collect it. Here, it is necessary to block out name labels or not use images in your reporting.

There still remains, however, the question of whether anonymity can really be protected as it could be possible to discern individuals even where measures have been taken to conceal identity. This can be particularly problematic where video is involved (Mortari & Harcourt, 2012). In practical terms, this can be solvable to some extent through the selection of images or sections of film as illustrative of the findings that you are presenting. If there are any distinct features of content, or content that may inappropriately disclose identity, then you should avoid using these in the presentation of your research outcomes.

It is also possible, as discussed by Allen (2015), that individuals do not want their data anonymised. This, in itself, creates its own ethical dilemmas as there is likely to be a contradiction between the awarding of formal ethical approval and your desire to adhere to the wishes of your participants. In the case of children in school, it is likely that you must ensure that you maintain secure, anonymised identification of your participants, particularly as, with children, they may not be able to predict how future use of the data could impact on them.

Outside of the direct content of images or artefacts, more generally, you may also be creating the opportunity for children to visibly (and potentially publicly) represent issues that are not ordinarily externalised (Bridger, 2013). This, therefore, creates the potential for your work to become intrusive rather than emancipatory (Aldridge, 2012), and care needs to be taken to mitigate against this. Working with teachers to ensure the exclusion of data that was not intended for research purposes can serve to safeguard in such instances.

The consideration of inadvertent representation of others, or issues, also highlights the needs of non-participants and ethical considerations that may be applied to broadening the moral duty that may be associated with your research. Particularly associated with any video-based research, careful attention as to who is included, and in what way, is needed. Extending such thoughts, Richardson (2019) calls us to heed those who are on the periphery of research but may still be affected by it. In instances where you select only some children to be involved, others may ask why they were not selected (Richardson, 2019). Therefore, explaining to whole groups about research that is taking place within them but using a smaller number of participants, particularly if there are external indicators such as cameras involved, is a sensitive approach to engage in.

Indeed, all of the tools of creative research described above have the potential to be 'public' in nature and will, in all instances, have an audience of some kind. Incorporating considerations of this into the way you structure and utilise data by thinking of the individual and group circumstances that you are working in can ensure these are managed so as not to unduly expose children to an audience they did not anticipate or create a sense of exclusion in particular circumstances.

Conclusion

This chapter has considered the tools that you may employ to support children's expression in creative approaches to research. Attending to children's cultures has been identified as effective in understanding expression, and giving choice in selection of tool, alongside the ability to manipulate the selected approach to convey meaning, has been explored. The need to ensure that children do not misconceive creative approaches to research as a judgement of artistry has been discussed. This has been explored in light of the natural proclivity children may have to provide linguistic support for visual data and graphic data in support of narrative expressions. Ultimately, the outcome for this as a researcher is a call to identify meaning and locate this within the intentions of participants. The section here also highlights the dynamic potential of creative approaches to research and explores ways within which this can be positively exploited.

You should now have an understanding that:

Tools in creative approaches to research can 'slow down' the thinking processes involved in responding to a research question and lead to considered responses
The complexities of creative tools can reflect the dimensions of experiences that are being conveyed
Participant control and researcher investment can generate a sense of value and collaboration in using these tools
In order to be effective, care needs to be taken to ensure an alignment of participant preferences and the potential of the approach selected

A key concern with all these methods is the need to ensure accurate interpretation. Each of them has potential, however, to ultimately generate a narrative of some kind to story children's experiences. In many instances it is appropriate to utilise artefacts as a segue into sense-making discussion. The following chapter focuses specifically on how we can ensure that the design, processes and outcomes associated with creative approaches research generate viable data for analysis. It addresses what we mean by the concept of viable data and how we situate the production of material artefacts that have been discussed here in relation to people and place. Consideration is given to the relationship between visual artefact and narrative data, and how these serve to support conceptual expression.

References

Aldridge, J. (2012). The participation of vulnerable children in photographic research. *Visual Studies*, 27(1), 48–58. doi:10.1080/1472586X.2012.642957.

Allen, L. (2015). Losing face? Photo-anonymisation and visual research integrity. *Visual Studies*, 30(3), 295–308. doi:10.1080/1472586X.2015.1016741.

Angell, R. J., & Angell, C. (2013). More than just 'snap crackle and pop'; 'draw, write and tell': an innovative research method with young children. *Journal of Advertising Research*, 13(1), 17–28.

Barriage, S., & Hicks, A. (2020). Mobile apps for visual research: affordances and challenges for participant-generated photography. *Library and Information Science Research*, 42(3). doi:10.1016/j.lisr.2020.101033.

Bridger, L. (2013). Seeing and telling households: a case for photo elicitation and graphic elicitation in qualitative research. *Graduate Journal of Social Science*, 10(2), 106–131.

Burkitt, E., Watling, D., & Cocks, F. (2019). Mixed emotion experiences for self or another person in adolescence. *Journal of Adolescence*, 75, 63–72.

Burkitt, E., Watling, D., & Message, H. (2019). Expressivity in children's drawings of themselves for adult audiences with varied authority and familiarity. *British Journal of Development Psychology*, 37, 354–368.

Carless, D., & Lam, R. (2014). The examined life: perspectives of lower primary school students in Hong Kong. *Education 3–13*, 42(3), 313–330.

Chesworth, L. (2016). A funds of knowledge approach to examining play interests: listening to children's and parents' perspectives. *International Journal of Early Years Education*, 24(3), 294–308. doi:10.1080/09669760.2016.1188370.

Culshaw, S. (2019). The unspoken power of collage? Using an innovative arts-based research method to explore the experience of struggling as a teacher. *London Review of Education*, 17(3), 268–283. doi:10.18546/LRE.17.3.03.

Drew, S., & Guillemin, M. (2014). From photographs to findings: visual meaning-making and interpretive engagement in the analysis of participant-generated images. *Visual Studies*, 29(1), 54–67. doi:10.1080/1472586X.2014.862994.

Fletcher, G. (2013). Of baby ducklings and clay pots: method and metaphor in HIV prevention. *Qualitative Health Research*, 23(11), 1551–1562.

Freeman, M., & Mathison, S. (2008). *Researching Children's Experiences*. New York: Guilford Publications.

Giguere, M. (2011). Social influences on the creative process: an examination of children's creativity and learning in dance. *International Journal of Education & the Arts*, 12(1.5), 1–13.

Harper, D. A. (2012). *Visual Sociology*. London and New York: Routledge.

Jewitt, C., Xambo, A., & Price, S. (2017). Exploring methodological innovation in the social sciences: the body in digital environments and the arts. *International Journal of Social Research Methodology*, 20(1), 105–120. doi:10.1080/13645579.2015.1129143.

Kara, H. (2015). *Creative Research Methods in the Social Sciences – A Practical Guide*. Bristol: Policy Press.

Ledin, P., & Machin, D. (2018). *Doing Visual Analysis – From Theory to Practice*. London: Sage.

Lipponen, L., Rajala, A., Hilppö, J., & Paananen, M. (2016). Exploring the foundations of visual methods used in research with children. *European Early Childhood Education Research Journal*, 24(6), 936–946. doi:10.1080/1350293X.2015.1062663.

Lodge, C. (2009). About face: visual research involving children, *Education 3–13*, 37(4), 361–370.

Luttrell, W. (2010). 'A camera is a big responsibility': a lens for analysing children's visual voices. *Visual Studies*, 25(3), 224–237. doi:10.1080/1472586X.2010.523274.

Mann, R., & Warr, D. (2017). Using metaphor and montage to analyse and synthesise diverse qualitative data: exploring the local worlds of 'early school leavers'. *International Journal of Social Research Methodology*, 20(6), 547–558. doi:10.1080/13645579.2016.1242316.

Mannay, D., Staples, E., & Edwards, V. (2017). Visual methodologies, sand and psychoanalysis: employing creative participatory techniques to explore the educational experiences of mature students and children in care. *Visual Studies*, 32(4), 345–358. doi:10.1080/1472586X.2017.1363636.

McCaffrey, T., & Edwards, J. (2015). Meeting art with art: arts-based methods enhance researcher reflexivity in research with mental health service users. *Journal of Music Therapy*, 52(4), 515–532.

Meager, N. (2017). Children make observational films – exploring a participatory visual method for art education. *International Journal of Education through Art*, 13(1), 7–22. doi:10.1386/eta.13.1.7_1.

Mortari, L., & Harcourt, D. (2012). 'Living' ethical dilemmas for researchers when researching with children. *International Journal of Early Years Education*, 20(3), 234–243. doi:10.1080/09669760.2012.715409.

Pithouse-Morgan, K., Van Laren, L., Singh, S., & Mudaly, R. (2013). Starting with ourselves in deepening our understanding of generativity in participatory educational research. *South African Journal of Education*, 33(4), 1–16.

Poynter, R. (2010). *The Handbook of Online and Social Media Research: Tools and Techniques for Market Researchers*. New York: Wiley.

Richardson, T. (2019). 'Why haven't I got one of those?' A consideration regarding the need to protect non-participant children in early years research. *European Early Childhood Education Research Journal*, 27(1), 5–14. doi:10.1080/1350293X.2018.1556530.

Rissanen, M.-J. (2020). Entangled photographers: agents and actants in preschoolers' photography talk. *International Journal of Education through Art*, 16(2), 271–286. doi:10.1386/eta_00031_1.

Roberts, A., & Woods, P. A. (2018). Theorising the value of collage in exploring educational leadership. *British Educational Research Journal*, 44(4), 626–642. doi:10.1002/berj.3451.

Rose, G. (2016). *Visual Methodologies: An Introduction to Researching With Visual Materials*, 4th ed. London: SAGE Publications.

Sanderud, J. R. (2020). Mutual experiences: understanding children's play in nature through sensory ethnography. *Journal of Adventure Education & Outdoor Learning*, 20(2), 111–122. doi:10.1080/14729679.2018.1557058.

Schulze, S. (2017). The value of two modes of graphic elicitation interviews to explore factors that impact on student learning in higher education. *Qualitative Sociology Review*, 13(2), 60–77.

Spencer, S. (2011). *Visual Research Methods in the Social Sciences: Awakening Visions*, 1st ed. New York: Routledge.

Swartz, S. (2011). 'Going deep' and 'giving back': strategies for exceeding ethical expectations when researching amongst vulnerable youth. *Qualitative Research*, 11(1), 47–68. doi:10.1177/1468794110385885.

Torre, D., & Murphy, J. (2015). A different lens: using photo-elicitation interviews in education research. *Education Policy Analysis Archives*, 23(111), 1–26.

Vaswani, N. (2018). Learning from failure: are practitioner researchers the answer when conducting research on sensitive topics with vulnerable children and young people? *International Journal of Social Research Methodology*, 21(4), 499–512.

Chapter 4

Generating viable data

> This belongs to Eluji Sontas – for club – totally private.
> (Julie, aged 11, diary entry)

This chapter will address concerns with what constitutes 'data' and what type of data can be generated through creative research methods. For example, the production of artefacts can readily be considered data in themselves, as can information generated through interview about them, and a combination of the two. However, further information regarding the context of either the production of the artefact or the experiences being conveyed can, and should, also be effectively utilised in research. This is hugely important when working with children as it is an often-overlooked aspect of data generation that significantly affects their engagement.

Key points for discussion will be:

- What constitutes viable data
- Situating the production of material artefacts – (audience, people and place)
- Sense of place in situating material artefacts
- Integrating narrative indicators
- Concrete artefacts and conceptual expression – generating narratives
- Ethical considerations

The generation of viable data in creative approaches to research concerns both the 'product' of the method and processes involved. So, our first question is, what do we actually mean by this?

What constitutes viable data

By product here I refer to a data outcome (usually a material artefact as discussed in Chapter 3) that can then be analysed in itself or used as a point of departure for the generation of further data. Each of these is multi-faceted, but an essential consideration is that prior to considering the complexity of the product, it can only be viable for analysis if the processes involved in its development are themselves secure and rigorous. Generally speaking, there are three aspects to this process that need to be considered; these concern your action as a researcher and the environment within which your working as geographically and socially significant.

Figure 4.1 models how the viability of the product of the method (whether this be photograph, film, diary etc.) is dependent upon the factors that have influenced its production as active processes. These are determined by your own action, the geographical location that you select and the social environment within which you conduct the research – each of these being within the concept of 'place of method', a broadly neglected consideration as an active contributing factor to research outcomes (Anderson, Adey, & Bevan, 2010).

What you do and say, and how you behave as 'a researcher', will inevitably affect how children respond to the research process. If you are an outsider to the research context, how you present yourself is significant; if you are researching an environment that you ordinarily operate in, how you integrate your role as researcher with your role as teacher/trainee/other professional will impact on children's response to you. The physical location, and human actors within it, will also shape children's interaction with the research method. These processes are significant in determining whether you have potentially viable data. Further to this, your product will only be viable if you can adequately analyse and interpret it.

Therefore, the product needs to be manageable and understandable. The following sections will consider each of these in turn to explore ways of ensuring the security of your research in the production and preparation of data that adequately addresses your research question. Processes need to ensure product viability, and you will have such data if this is reflective of your research intentions.

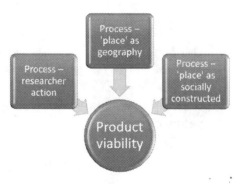

Figure 4.1 Ensuring product viability

> **Thinking points**
>
> How might you answer the following questions based on the environment that you intend to conduct your research in:
>
> What considerations would you need to take into account when conducting research in the school context(s) you are working in?
> Which physical spaces are available to you?
> What meaning might these physical spaces have for your child participants?
> Who might have access to your 'place of method'?
> How might this create an 'audience' for your participants?

Creative forms of enquiry, particularly those that use arts-based methods, are considered potentially stimulating for all parties involved, including participants themselves and audiences (McCaffrey & Edwards, 2015). The complexity of non-verbal data, however, presents us with a challenge in terms of how we might analyse our findings. Chapter 3 addressed the types of data that might be generated. The analysis of such complex information is less than straightforward, and can be dependent upon the processes used to generate the data and the environment in which this occurs. The very basis on which creative approaches to research are justified (individual, subjective, polysemic) serve to set challenges here. This arises from there being a lack of uniformity in data responses, which means there is a greater emphasis placed on interpretation by the researcher than may appear to be the case in other approaches to research. Inevitably, this also results in concerns regarding the academic rigour of such investigations.

In terms of considering how viable data can be generated, there are some considerations here that will need to theme your work throughout. I consider the concept of 'viable' data to be that which is usable for the research purposes. Within the framework of Figure 4.1, as the methodology of place, and how this impacts on the production of data, it is first of value to consider how we ensure that research is both 'valid' and 'reliable'. I deliberately set these latter two terms in inverted commas to acknowledge that they are moot concepts in the light of creative approaches to research.

Traditionally in research, under the dominance of positivist orientations to studies where there is a single representation of reality being explored, investigations needed to demonstrate that they were measuring data that answered the question being asked (validity) and that a study could be adequately replicated with further populations (reliability) (Cohen, Manion, & Morrison, 2017; Lincoln & Denzin, 2011). This is a logically followed, 'neat' expectation of research design and frequently appears in preparation for dissertation work at all levels. However, when it comes to creative approaches to research, this becomes much more challenging. As identified

58 Generating viable data

above, part of the purpose of using the tools that we are discussing here is that they can reflect the complexity of children's experiences, as the concept of creativity is in itself undeniably complex (Kara, 2015). This is innovative within the broader history of research, which is widely considered positive (Nind & Vinha, 2016). The question here, however, is how we can make rigour in the research process manageable?

At this point, I think it is helpful to draw on aspects of Lincoln and Guba's quality criteria for qualitative research. This has been utilised by other authors who work with arts-based research (see, for example, Kara, 2015), as it proposes a conceptualisation of what ensures quality in particularly divergent approaches to research, i.e. as in creativity where expansion of ideas forms an essential part of the purpose. The application of the ideas of validity and reliability have come to be defined as exploring the 'trustworthiness' of the research, and consists of processes to establish credibility (can you be confident that what is being presented is 'true'), transferability (can what you've found be applied to other contexts), dependability (are your findings consistent and could they be repeated) and confirmability (are you sure you are representing the actual views of your participants and not what you want their views to be?) (Lincoln & Guba, 1985). These apply largely to the analysis of data but are also essential to bear in mind in the preparation of your data, as underpinning each of these factors will be a need to be critically self-reflective throughout your work (McCaffrey & Edwards, 2015).

For example, if we think about the idea of credibility, within the context of research in schools with children it is important to think about what the perceptions of other children and their teachers may be. On a practical note, were you to share your findings informally, what would the comments of your colleagues/peers be? I emphasise this because it is easy to assume that if you are to appear credible you need to reinforce pre-existing ideas, and much educational research has been criticised as having a tendency to do this. Therefore, you need to think about the evidence you are generating and how you have interpreted this – in the case of working in schools it is helpful to actually share this with practitioners, and this can sometimes answer concerns very simply.

Scenario

To be honest I was struggling a bit about the credibility part of what you said to think about – one of the children had drawn themselves outside, clearly at night which didn't really make sense but seemed really clear in the picture – I hadn't spoken to the child yet but was trying to figure out from the picture what it meant – I'd asked the children to draw a picture 'how I relax at home' – I asked the class teacher if I could run this past him and we sat down and had a chat – it turns out that he's of Eastern European heritage and his local community socialises in this way – I felt bad that this was a surprise to me but it made sense then.

This checking of what appears to be credible during the research process enhances the quality of the continuing research, thus ensuring rigour in terms of checking what may/may not be viable to retain for analysis. So, in order to generate trustworthy data (in preparation for your trustworthy analysis), revisiting and questioning as you progress is a helpful approach to take.

Situating the production of material artefacts – (audience, people and place)

If we are basing justification for using creative approaches to research as a means to ensure representation and inclusivity (Lomax, 2012), then one question for us to consider is how to protect, as far as is possible, the integrity of our data generation process. This section considers how we might do this by setting an environment for data production that is as favourable as possible to support self-expression of children. One of the first considerations to make here will be the people that will see these representations, as first discussed in Chapter 3.

Children are known to feel freer in self-expression when they know their audience (Burkitt, Watling, & Message, 2019). As you will be a key member of the 'audience' to which children are expressing themselves, it is important that you take time to get to know them before engaging in research, unless your research topic would particularly suggest otherwise. It is also crucial to remain aware that any other individual who is present during the production of the artefact, or whom the children perceive may become aware of their drawing/photograph, also forms an 'audience' for the child and may affect their approach to what they are doing. This is addressing the social aspects of research environments and how they affect your study, as where your participants are producing artefacts to represent experience are never neutral environments (Lipponen, Rajala, Hilppö, & Paananen, 2016).

Therefore, it is wise during the research process to take advantage of all of the information you may be able to access to help understand what may be 'going on' for the children. This includes observing and listening carefully as children create their artefacts, whether this be in a whole class environment, small group or individual context, in your presence. Understanding complete experiences are dependent on linking both the visual and audible. The narratives that can accompany children's drawings/modelling can serve to be a valuable source of information and evolve as the artefact is produced. It can therefore make sense for you to deliberately engage in speaking informally with children as they produce their artefacts. This will serve as both a relationship builder and also a way for you to potentially access internal narratives (about the artefact and its focus) and external narratives (concerning the social environment within which it is being produced) (Freeman & Mathison, 2008). This generates additional data that can be used in conjunction with subsequent interviews and data analysis.

Following this technique is something that I have found helpful with children of primary school age, as ensuring that you are present as they respond to the research task appears to add value to the process. It works on the level described above and also serves to support the way that younger children in particular appreciate your engagement. This can be achieved by moving around a whole class, for example as they draw, gaining snippets of information. Having children draw all together is sometimes a pragmatic decision based on the ability to 'disturb' children in school but also has value in terms of providing supporting data for interpretation.

Such narratives can operate at different levels – from basic descriptions of what is being made to more complex representations of lived experience (Coates & Coates, 2011). It can also, very simply, act as a further conduit for conversation:

SE: Hi Lucy – how are you doing today?
LUCY: Good thanks – we've just been out playing
SE: Ah, yeah – I saw you – it looked like you were playing 'octopus' (a free play game created and played by the 'whole class')
LUCY: Yeah everyone joins in –
SE: Actually, you were chatting about that when you were doing your drawing the other day …
LUCY: Yeah, it's 'cos you asked us to show what we liked doing at playtime …
SE: I think you were saying that you chose to draw that 'cos everyone can join in …
LUCY: I did – you can see the people here … (pointing at her picture)
SE: I can – can you tell me a bit more about what everyone's doing?

As indicated in Chapter 3, with children of secondary school age it would be unwise to ask them to produce any artefact in a context that is in front of their peers – in most schools attempts to do this would (in my experience) create tensions of unintended 'hierarchies of cool' (Fitton, Read, Horton, Little, Toth, & Guo, 2012). This may mean that you would either fail to invoke a genuine representation or that responses are skewed to what is deemed socially desirable. It also creates the possibility of further consequences for particular children outside of the research environment if others judge them on what they have produced. This is not to say that it would be entirely unproblematic in primary schools, but just that as a general guideline, this is worth considering. It avoids some of the concerns that, in relation to research, an expression of taste can affect children's acceptance or otherwise within a group (Lomax, 2012). It also helps support the expression of more genuine perspectives, as open, 'public' scenarios may enhance children's tendency to draw culturally acceptable images (O'Sullivan & Macphail, 2010) rather than what they would really like to convey.

This may be particularly enhanced if speaking about more sensitive topics. In such situations it is more appropriate for you to ensure that you spend time with children individually rather than as groups, as they construct their artefact. This enables you to ask questions as the artefact is made as described above and means that there is a possibility of asking questions in an environment that feels constructive and avoids any sense of being in a testing situation (Wiseman, Rossmann, Lee, & Harris, 2019). It can also be helpful as some discussions come to include more sensitive topics as the research evolves. Abbie (aged 8yrs) was chatting as she was constructing a model of her doing her homework:

> I'm trying to do this with us all in it ... this is me with my reading book ... we're sometimes all there together ... my Dad likes us to be together all around the table ... I'm doing my Mum now ... it's a bit tricky 'cos sometimes she's not usually there ... I'm going to do my uncle now ... he's got special needs so he lives with us so we can help him ...
>
> (Abbie, aged 8yrs)

Abbie's narrative as she was creating her model identified a complex homelife that affected her engagement with school. I was able to ask her about some of the points that she made at the time, while others I talked to her about later, after I had come to understand more about her background. In order to adequately interpret the data that was being produced here I needed to understand, for example, what she meant by 'sometimes she's not usually there' and the significance of this. I gained the additional information by speaking to her class teacher – what this also did was identify what would and would not be appropriate to discuss with her when we later met.

Sense of place in situating material artefacts

This leads us to consider how we ensure we conduct research in an appropriate place in terms of location. Where data is produced can significantly affect what is produced (Gagnon, Jacob, & McCabe, 2015). This refers to the social aspects of space, geographical and temporal (the 'where' to the 'when'). The discussion above refers to aspects of the social space as affecting your research – this section explores these further in light of how you are conducting your research in schools as institutional settings.

The sense of place when conducting research in schools requires consideration on several levels. The first, and most straightforward, is the school as an environment that operates on clear scheduling with timetables, room size and subjects that will inevitably frame your research. These factors can also be seen to compromise the research (Anderson et al., 2010) as you may (will) not always have control over where and when the research takes place. This also combines with the fact that, on occasion, this schedule is disrupted by unanticipated change, or change that you perhaps had not been informed of. This has implications for your research design and approach on days you are in school. If we start with the latter, it is important that you remain flexible – you may get to school and find that your participants are delayed as the school assembly went on longer than expected due to an incident that took place on the premises the previous evening that had to be addressed, or perhaps one of the school buses broke down on the morning journey and the children you were due to be working with have not yet arrived. These are just illustrations of possibilities that are not unusual in a school context.

The key message here is that these things will happen, and it is rare that a research project of any significance goes entirely smoothly. This is the reality of conducting studies in school, and therefore maintaining a flexible mindset is hugely helpful. Planning ahead in order to allow time to revisit the school, if not one you are working in, following any delayed work is also a wise thing to do.

These kinds of considerations are consistent with Anderson et al.'s (2010) suggestion that as researchers we should consider our approach as a 'polylogue' where we think about not only ourselves and our participants but also 'place' in terms of the location in which the research occurs. Very often, the location of research is 'neutralised' – it is identified as a factor that is minimised but, in practice, it can be very significant. Very often we will see descriptions of locations for research that say they are carried out, for example, away from the class but within the sight of the teacher (Burkitt et al., 2019; Everley & Everley, 2018). However, space, as social, physical and temporal, is hugely 'active' in its impact on what you do – both enabling and constraining (Anderson et al., 2010), and these are essential considerations to make. For most of my time researching I have been guilty of neutralising the concept of space both in terms of what I have actually done and what I have subsequently written, identifying that I have selected areas that are familiar to children and ones in which we will not be disturbed, but in which we are close enough to the teacher/other appropriate adult to ensure child protection. It was not until more recently that I have come to consider the place of method as really impactful on what I do in school and its having significant impact on the spatiality of 'methodological praxis' (Anderson et al., 2010, p590).

Considering school environments, it is also important to think about the temporal aspect of conducting research in relation to space as 'place'. The classroom is very different during timetabled sessions, break times and after school, meaning you may have the same space but with different meaning. I would therefore add this to Anderson et al.'s (2010) assessment of concepts of space for our purposes here. Geographically, too, there can be a sense of privilege associated with accessing certain areas in school that children are not normally permitted to enter. An example might be working with children in a common room area not normally used by their year group. This was something I did with early work where children kept diaries. They wrote their entries in their own time away from school (suggested reasons for this are discussed in Chapter 2), but I met with them once a week to discuss key issues they had raised and also to maintain engagement. This gave a sense of belonging to the children involved. In evaluating the research approach, one child commented:

> It's been good doing this 'cos you feel like you've been chosen and its special – you're sort of in a team 'cos you're listening to us all – it's cool being here too – we can go in here to see you but we're not normally allowed.
>
> (Conor, aged 12yrs)

Another wrote at the front of her diary:

> This belongs to Eluji Sontas – for club – totally private.
>
> (Julie, aged 11, diary entry)

The concept of belonging to a club was not necessarily the sense that I had set out to create but it was one that can clearly be incorporated into group work. The choice of space had given value to the research and, as it took place at a time when no other children were around, served to facilitate and support discussion, meaning that contributors knew their ideas were being taken seriously and the data, therefore, was potentially more detailed.

In this instance, choice of space (geographical, social and temporal) enhanced the method. But I have also had instances where my choice was not so successful. The scenario box that follows describes a situation where I had chosen a setting that was protected from influence by one group but not another, and this proved significant in negatively affecting the production of viable data.

Scenario

I was working with children on an individual basis in a primary school where participants were writing key words or drawing images associated with their conceptualisation of 'health'. This was completed in the classroom when the rest of the class were elsewhere in a music lesson. There were no other children present to affect participant engagement and other children would not have entered the room at a time when the class teacher was not present. However, it was a space that was accessible to support staff; in this particular instance, a teaching assistant who had supported this participant entered the room – on seeing this child writing she noted that he was not forming letters as they had been practicing and verbally reprimanded him for this. The intervention meant that the child immediately looked uncomfortable and ceased writing.

Thinking about the place of method, the following questions may help you locate your work:

Thinking points

Think about how you might answer the following questions, considering the place of method in your selected research school.

> What is the social context of your choice?
> Will this remain static during the period of data collection or do you need to anticipate any potential change?
> What meaning might the space/place have for your participants?
> Is the scheduling of your work appropriate to the social and geographic context of the space?
> How might all of the above affect the viability of the data that you generate?

A final consideration to make here is the recording of some of the additional information that can be used to support the viability of your data as described above. This can be included in your field notes, and can provide invaluable data in itself and help support your interpretation of the main outcomes of your work that you carry out directly in school.

Attending to concepts of space in your research highlights the importance of maintaining records of all aspects of your work. Doing this can add to the richness of data. By 'richness' in this context I am referring to the complexity in terms of additional dimensions of information that can later be used in analysis (see Chapters 2 and 7). This would therefore mean recording silences and non-verbal responses (Chesworth, 2016), and also incidental comments made by children or yourself in the environments described above. This latter point forms part of your own reflections that should take place throughout your research. This is discussed in detail in Chapter 7, but an acknowledgement of your own behaviours and comments alongside responses of children can be helpful. This kind of information also helps you remain focused on your task and maintain an awareness of your interactions with participants. Included here are the factors that surround your actual research that may affect your work but do not form a direct part of it. Ensuring that you record this information in field notes creates what I would term 'potential data' – it acts as a record for your own purposes but can also be data in itself. The more comprehensive this is, the better, as you may not recognise at the time something that later proves to be significant. Essentially, you need to ensure that you have information that may help you address any anomalies that you may find in your data when you come to your analysis.

Integrating narrative indicators

One feature of children's diaries was that they would sometimes use meta-narratives in their entries. As a term that ordinarily refers to narrative about a narrative, I use it here to refer to visual indicators that children include in their diaries that are in addition to the words in the main text. Narratives in a general sense operate as an instrument of the mind in the construction of reality (Bruner, 1986). As indicated in Chapter 3, when children keep diaries this will tend to be a very 'live' document in the sense that they will add particular meta-narratives to create emphasis. These may take the form, for example, of the use of capital letters, highlighted words and additional notes as they revisit entries that they have made. These will need to be integrated to form a whole narrative in order for you to analyse the data and you will need to decipher the meaning of each. It is important that these additional features are acknowledged and integrated into the meaning of what children are presenting. Sometimes these are straightforward:

> I find that Mr Mitchell goes a little bit OVER THE TOP!
> (Alison, aged 13yrs, diary entry)

At other times, entries can be a little harder to interpret. Megan made the following diary entry:

> It's really unfair that Mr Casey always favours some people over others. He always asks the same people to answer his questions …
> (Megan, aged 15yrs, diary entry)

The following week she then returned to the entry and in the margin added:

> Well, I don't know what I'm moaning about actually. He's strict but he is fair and he's actually a good teacher so I shouldn't really say bad things about him.
> (Megan, aged 15yrs, diary entry)

So, the question was, did this meta-narrative inserted around the original text mean that she meant the latter rather than the former, or that she meant each point at the time? Was the intention that it was an 'overnarrative' that supersedes the original entry? Or did it just indicate that she had become concerned that the teacher may access her diary? In these instances, it is clear that further information is required to analyse what has been said. Therefore, as for images that may be polysemic, a further narrative needs to be constructed with the participants to ensure an accurate understanding. This narrative can then be used in conjunction with the text in the analysis process.

Concrete artefacts and conceptual expression – generating narratives

Indeed, arguments around the value of producing artefacts in the research process are frequently focused on the way in which they can be used to convey concepts in ways that are more accessible to children because of their cultural relevance (as discussed in Chapter 2). It is also clear that children are aware themselves of their ability to communicate through visual forms. Children as young as the age of 3yrs are considered to have the potential capacity to convey meaning through drawing, and this becomes more sophisticated as they become older to very specifically convey perspectives and emotions through their drawings (Burkitt et al., 2019).

The data that you generate using the tools that we have discussed earlier in this text are each usable in their own right, and part of their value is to circumvent the need to verbally articulate experience. These should suffice (Blodget et al., 2013), particularly if the above measures have been employed to avoid compromising any subsequent analysis (Burkitt et al., 2019). However, as you will have seen from the content of this book, it is often helpful to facilitate verbal explanation and expansion by your participants. This enables you to verify meaning and extend your own understanding. It is also the opportunity for further detailing by participants consistent with Coates and Coates (2011) argument that these elements are inextricable in ensuring understanding if the intention of our research is to understand experience. In my experience, it is therefore important that you include interviews of some kind in order to create a minimal data set for each child.

If we are seeking to understand experience, then speaking to children allows us to deal with any limitations in the skilfulness of children that may obscure the meaning in their artefact. It also helps overcome any frustrations children may have had if they felt unable to fully manipulate the selected tool in the way they would have hoped. This may appear to contradict earlier arguments that one of the values of using creative visual approaches to research lies in its non-verbal nature, however, the artefacts retain all of the characteristics that are sought in experiential research and serve as a conduit through which you as a researcher can help co-construct an understanding of the children's intentions. In some instances, this means you can create a comprehensive internal narrative for analysis, in others, children's responses will be less complex but will, nevertheless, serve to mitigate against assumptions that we may be tempted to make as researchers. Therefore, this essential data set can be enhanced by field notes as described earlier, but, as identified in Chapter 2, it is an absolute minimum for the type of research that we are discussing here that you ensure you have interpreted the creative data in the way intended by the child.

Ethical considerations

Reflecting on the content of this chapter, data is only viable if it has been ethically generated. Some ethical considerations when working with children to produce viable data are anticipated as a matter of course and included in your consent procedures (Aldridge, 2012). By these factors I refer to issues such as gaining participant consent/assent, parental consent, ensuring anonymity and right to withdraw etc. Some ethical considerations are less evident but have been touched on in this chapter, and particularly concern those that emerge within the research process. Essentially, it is important to view ethical processes as continuing phenomena to ensure the continued creation of safe spaces in which children can ask questions and gain confirmation of expectations as they work through the research (Arnott, Martinez-Lejarreta, Wall, Blaisdell, & Palaiologou, 2020).

Things to consider, and aligned with this, could be the dynamics of group selection and organisation if working with groups of children. Ethical tensions continually arise in the multiple relationships that exist in the research context (Gallacher & Gallagher, 2008; Graham, Powell, & Taylor, 2015). Questions you may need to address could be included in the following: how will you ensure that children maintain one another's confidence? How will you address issues children may have when another adult comes into your research space unexpectedly? If you are working with a whole class, how will you manage situations where children or their parent/guardian have not given consent to join you? If a child appears to be beginning to disclose information that you had not anticipated and that seems to be of a sensitive nature, do you find a way of guiding them in another direction or do you allow them to continue with what they are telling you? These are all questions that will need to be answered on a context-specific basis, but if you have thought about the possibilities beforehand, and sought the advice of adults responsible for ordinarily working with the children (if this is not you), then you will be much better equipped to cope sensitively with these outcomes. These form part of the ethics of care that pertain to your behaviours in relation to those involved in your work (Mortari & Harcourt, 2012).

When considering the practicalities of completing your study, particularly where you are asking children to produce artefacts in a 'public' scenario of some kind, it can be difficult to initiate what they are doing — for children to 'get going' on the task. Some authors suggest that it is appropriate to take a persuasive stance in supporting participants in producing artefacts as data (Freeman & Mathison, 2008). If you come across such recommendations, do think carefully about whether this is appropriate for your situation. Give children space to respond first and then decide if you need, or if it is appropriate, to persuade. If children display any indicators that they are resistant to taking part, allow them the freedom to refuse consent/assent in practical terms by simply not responding. This avoids the need to explain a desire to withdraw in a context that potentially incorporates perceived inequality in power distribution, making children reluctant to speak out (Slepičková & Bartošová, 2014) — even if they have already formally agreed to take part. Their understanding of what you expected may not be complete or they may have agreed to take part to please their teacher (especially if this is you!) — as an 'insider' this is a particularly challenging ethical issue (Vaswani, 2018). The presence of someone else in the class or discomfort with the setting may also affect how they feel, and provide reasons why children might need to cease their engagement.

Attention needs to be paid as to whether you may think a child is participating from a sense of compulsion (Gallacher & Gallagher, 2008) — you need to be very aware of this. Sensitising yourself to your research context and responding to any indication of concern from the children you are working with will help support you in making sound ethical decisions as you carry out your research.

Conclusion

This chapter has considered what we mean by generating viable data. It has covered some topics specific to the nuances of working with children in school environments that may not be covered in more formalised methodology textbooks, largely because, very often, working with children in a practical sense fails to follow 'textbook' advice. Working in school environments is a challenging business, and even when you plan meticulously, things can sometimes happen that seem to conspire against you. If they do, make sure you maintain your optimism, as all of these events are informing you about the real lives of your participants.

Viable data has been explained as that which has been ethically generated and can be analysed. It includes the consideration of the socio-cultural environments of the school and location of the research. Acknowledgement is given to the actions of you as a researcher within what is a dynamic, physical and social environment. It further highlights the need to integrate your wider observations into the production of data. This locates interpretation as an ongoing, negotiated process.

Having considered the methodological place for your research and vagaries of geographical, social and temporal locations of conducting your investigations with children, you should now have an understanding that:

Viable data is that which has sufficient integrity to be analysed and interpreted
Viable data is produced in a rigorous, ethically sound environment
Viability is dependent upon your assessment of the school as sense of place in terms of geography and social environment, and as influenced by your action as a researcher and the temporal location of your research

Essentially, then, what you should be able to do following the processes above is create a data set that can be analysed. The specific questions that you need to ask in your interviews to ensure accurate interpretation of data are explored in Chapter 6.

Key elements of ensuring an approach that safeguards research integrity with children are issues of power and expression. The following chapter considers how this operates in a research context and suggests ways that creative approaches can mitigate against issues associated with the distribution of power. It explores how you mitigate against the relatively powerful position that is assumed to abide in adult researchers. As power here is considered not an absolute phenomenon it can be renegotiated to ensure potential empowerment of children. Additionally, attention is given to particular circumstances regarding participants and research topics that may impact on your research.

References

Aldridge, J. (2012). The participation of vulnerable children in photographic research. *Visual Studies*, 27(1), 48–58. doi:10.1080/1472586X.2012.642957.

Anderson, J., Adey, P., & Bevan, P. (2010). Positioning place: polylogic approaches to research methodology. *Qualitative Research*, 10(5),589–604.

Arnott, L., Martinez-Lejarreta, L., Wall, K., Blaisdell, C., & Palaiologou, I. (2020). Reflecting on three creative approaches to informed consent with children under six. *British Educational Research Journal*, 46(4), 786–810. doi:10.1002/berj.3619.

Blodget, A., Coholic, D., Schinke, R., McGannon, K., Peltier, D., & Pheasant, C. (2013). Moving beyond words: exploring the use of an arts based research method in Aboriginal community sport, *Qualitative Research in Sport, Exercise and Health*, 5(3), 312–331.

Bruner, J. S. (1986). *Actual Minds, Possible Worlds*. Cambridge, MA: Harvard University Press.

Burkitt, E., Watling, D., & Message, H. (2019). Expressivity in children's drawings of themselves for adult audiences with varied authority and familiarity. *British Journal of Developmental Psychology*, 37(3), 354–368. doi:10.1111/bjdp.12278.

Chesworth, L. (2016). A funds of knowledge approach to examining play interests: listening to children's and parents' perspectives. *International Journal of Early Years Education*, 24(3), 294–308. doi:10.1080/09669760.2016.1188370.

Coates, E., & Coates, A. (2011). The subjects and meanings of young children's drawings. In D. Faulkner & E. Coates (Eds.), *Exploring Children's Creative Narratives* (pp. 115–139). ebook: Taylor & Francis.

Cohen, L., Manion, L., & Morrison, K. (2017). *Research Methods in Education*, 8th Ed. London: Routledge.

Everley, S., & Everley, K. (2018). Primary school children's experiences of physical activity: the place of social and cultural capital in participation and implications for schools. *Early Child Development and Care*, 189(12), 2032–2042. doi:10.1080/03004430.2018.1431231.

Fitton, D., Read, J. C., Horton, M., Little, L., Toth, N., & Guo, Y. (2012). Constructing the cool wall: a tool to explore teen meanings of cool. *PsychNology Journal*, 10(2), 141–162.

Freeman, M., & Mathison, S. (2008). *Researching Children's Experiences*. New York: Guilford Publications.

Gagnon, M., Jacob, J. D., & McCabe, J. (2015). Locating the qualitative interview: reflecting on space and place in nursing research. *Journal of Research in Nursing*, 20(3), 203–215. doi:10.1177/1744987114536571.

Gallacher, L. A., & Gallagher, M. (2008). Methodological immaturity in childhood research? Thinking through 'participatory methods'. *Childhood*, 15(4), 499–516.

Graham, A., Powell, M. A., & Taylor, N. (2015). Ethical research involving children. *Family Matters*, (96), 23–28.

Kara, H. (2015). *Creative Research Methods in the Social Sciences – A Practical Guide*. Bristol: Policy Press.

Lincoln, Y. S., & Denzin, N. K. (2011). *The Sage Handbook of Qualitative Research*, 4th Ed. Thousand Oaks, CA: Sage.

Lincoln, Y. S., & Guba, E. G. (1985). *Naturalistic Inquiry*. Newbury Park, CA: Sage Publications.

Lipponen, L., Rajala, A., Hilppö, J., & Paananen, M. (2016). Exploring the foundations of visual methods used in research with children. *European Early Childhood Education Research Journal*, 24(6), 936–946. doi:10.1080/1350293X.2015.1062663.

Lomax, H. (2012). Contested voices? Methodological tensions in creative visual research with children. *International Journal of Social Research Methodology*, 15(2), 105–117. doi:10.1080/13645579.2012.649408.

McCaffrey, T., & Edwards, J. (2015). Meeting art with art: arts-based methods enhance researcher reflexivity in research with mental health service users. *Journal of Music Therapy*, 52(4), 515–532. doi:10.1093/jmt/thv016.

Mortari, L., & Harcourt, D. (2012). 'Living' ethical dilemmas for researchers when researching with children. *International Journal of Early Years Education*, 20(3), 234–243. doi:10.1080/09669760.2012.715409.

Nind, M., & Vinha, H. (2016). Creative interactions with data: using visual and metaphorical devices in repeated focus groups. *Qualitative Research*, 16(1), 9.

O'Sullivan, M., & Macphail, A. (2010). *Young People's Voices in PE and Youth Sport*. London: Routledge.

Slepičková, L., & Bartošová, M. K. (2014). Ethical and methodological associations in doing research on children in a school environment. *New Educational Review*, 38(4), 84–93.

Vaswani, N. (2018). Learning from failure: are practitioner researchers the answer when conducting research on sensitive topics with vulnerable children and young people? *International Journal of Social Research Methodology*, 21(4), 499–512. doi:10.1080/13645579.2018.1434866.

Wiseman, N., Rossmann, C., Lee, J., & Harris, N. (2019). 'It's like you are in the jungle': using the draw-and-tell method to explore preschool children's play preferences and factors that shape their active play. *Health Promotion Journal of Australia*, 30(S1), 85–94.

Chapter 5

The nature of power and empowerment

> How are you claiming that you're empowering children? Do they even care about what you're doing?
>
> (Conference delegate question)

This chapter will explore the nature of power relations that exist between researcher/researched and adult/child. It will consider arguments that creative approaches to research are empowering for participants (Swartz, 2011) with respect to ownership and control of the research direction. It will also consider the limitations of this, particularly with respect to whether taking part in certain research can, in itself, be empowering for participants either in terms of process or outcome. It will therefore challenge the very place that research with children and young people actually has within social sciences. The role of the teacher(s)/other gatekeepers and affect they may have on this process will also be considered. It takes a Foucauldian stance on the concept of power as a negotiated and negotiable phenomenon (Foucault & Gordon, 1980).

Key points for discussion will be:

- Researching vulnerable groups
- Researching sensitive subjects
- The contested nature of 'empowerment'
- Relational empowerment
- Empowerment in focus of concern
- Empowerment in research as process
- Empowerment and ownership of interpretation
- Ethical considerations

The relationship that exists between control of the production of knowledge and the holding of power is profound (Freeman & Mathison, 2008). If we are considering the ways in which knowledge is constructed around and about children's experiences through research, there is an inevitable hierarchical structure in terms of the researcher as privileged outsider (Delph-Janiurek, 2001). I therefore seek to address some of the considerations that you may need

72 The nature of power and empowerment

to make in your research to ensure that the assumed empowerment that exists in rhetoric surrounding creative approaches is actually realised in your work.

Before progressing, it is perhaps worthwhile considering what your conception of power is in order to then engage with different scenarios within which the phenomenon may be addressed in research:

> **Thinking points**
>
> Consider how you might answer the following questions:
>
> What do you understand by the concept of power?
> Do you consider power to be absolute or negotiable?
> How might power differentials affect the way that children as participants respond to you as a researcher?

Researching vulnerable groups

In much research, it is considered axiomatic that all children as participants are necessarily considered 'vulnerable'. Indeed, ethical approval processes categorise individuals under the age of 18yrs in this way, as do ethical guidelines for research more broadly (BERA, 2018). However, when working with children in school, there are a range of different vulnerabilities that may be experienced, and which require careful consideration.

The concept of vulnerability is highly complex and there is little agreement as to how it is constituted (Bracken-Roche et al., 2017). Essentially, though, in research, a vulnerability necessarily projects differentials in power to the disadvantage of the participant. Considering the ways in which vulnerabilities arise, this may be due to issues concerning the children themselves, where they are formally identified as being vulnerable through the education system, or perhaps such vulnerability emanates from the challenging situation in which the child lives within their home context. However, there may also be particular concerns regarding the environments, particularly social, that they may be working in, including the contexts that you may wish to create as a researcher in order to conduct your investigation. This is because it is arguable that children may be made vulnerable through the actual research process. Considering your research approach, this therefore has dual implications – firstly in terms of the way in which you seek to ensure adequate representation of children and also with respect to how you ensure adequate protection.

The model shown in Figure 5.1 illustrates the considerations that researchers need to make with respect to the children they are working with. The vulnerable child here refers to all participants that you involve in your study.

In this figure, the child, as vulnerable participant, is placed at the centre of considerations. All of the decisions that you make should serve to 'maximise

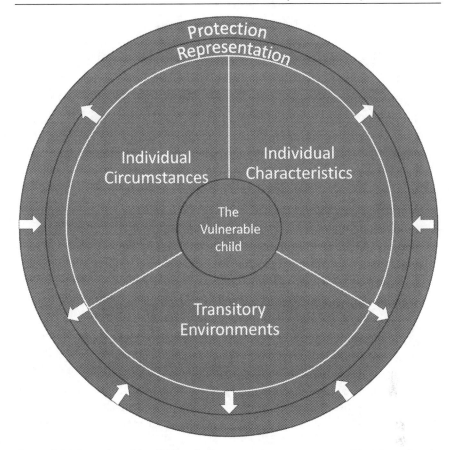

Figure 5.1 The vulnerable child and the research process – considerations for the researcher

benefits and minimise harm' (BERA, 2018). Around each child then, we have considerations of their individual characteristics and circumstances, and the transitory environments that they may find themselves in. The inner circle surrounds these considerations to convey how each of these need to be used to inform how the child can represent their experiences. The outer circle, surrounding the whole, is the environment of protection that needs to be provided for children to do this safely.

The individual characteristics of a child that you may be working with will largely be those that affect the relationship between you and their interaction with the methods that you are selecting to conduct your research. This determines, in the first instance, how you manage the power relations between yourself and your participant, as will later be discussed in this chapter, or the essential tools that you employ. As identified in Chapter 3, this may mean working with children where they face challenges in manipulation, either because of age or Special Educational Needs and Disabilities (SEND). Simply switching materials, from plasticine to play doh, for example, solved the problem of children creating the model that they wanted to use to represent their experiences.

With respect to individual circumstances, challenging situations or environments that children experience outside of school may directly affect the way in which they can engage in the research process. They may also affect the way in which school is engaged with by the child more widely. For example, children from traveller communities have been identified as being reluctant to share work of a performative nature and have a sense that they matter less than other children (Cudworth, 2008; Daniels, 2008). Their culture challenges some dominant values promoted in formal education environments (Gómez, Padrós, Ríos, Mara, & Pukepuke, 2019). In terms of the implications such factors have for you as a researcher, this will very much depend on the nature of their challenges and the plans that the school have in place to support the child. There may, for example, be certain triggers that can be problematic for individuals, or there could be particular topics or comments that need to be avoided by you as you engage with your participants. As will apply to all such situations, you will need to work closely with staff who understand the complexities of considerations that you need to make. Generally speaking, proactively seeking out the advice of the class teacher or others responsible for any child you are working with is welcomed, and establishing positive relationships leads to continued support and clearer safeguarding for your participants.

Throughout the process it is also important to acknowledge that authorities working with children who are formally identified as vulnerable will have their best interests prioritised, but that each may have a different perspective on the nature of these priorities (Munro, Holmes, & Ward, 2005) or how they may affect your approach as a researcher. Mannay, Staples and Edwards (2017) identify that the links between the internal 'world' of individuals from marginalised communities and shared social worlds is a crucial consideration when conducting research.

One technique that can be used is to share your own experience with children that you are working with in your research. Swartz (2011) utilised this approach and found that vulnerable teenagers were placed at ease as a result, and felt more able to share their perspectives in her research. This would appear a positive outcome with evident elements of a shared enterprise and democratic endeavour. Such practice within a school environment would come with a note of caution, however; sharing of experience will not be an evenly distributed exchange – you will still be the adult and researcher and you control the subsequent analysis and interpretation of data that your participants generate. You are still arriving having had the permissions and associated implicit or explicit approval of gatekeepers within that educational establishment. As discussed in the final section of this chapter, the ethical context of encouraging sharing of sometimes personal information, particularly from vulnerable groups, carries with it a great deal of responsibility.

A further technique that can reduce difference is one of laughter and sharing humour (Delph-Janiurek, 2001). If it suits your personality, do not be afraid to relax with children and have fun in what you are doing. This creates a sense of shared endeavour and positivity as you co-construct your understanding of experience. It is worth considering here, also, your positionality as a researcher, which may affect your relations with children (Gormally & Coburn, 2014). Essentially, within research, this usually involves your gender and race that is 'declared' when you write up your work, but is also a relational factor that may impact on the power relations that children experience with you. However, your positionality is also affected by your values and declaring these to your participants can facilitate the establishment of a sense of shared endeavour that can reduce power differentials between you and your participants.

The above largely concerns children's vulnerabilities within individual circumstances. As such, they are generally characterised by a perception of difference and are therefore relational. This means that your approach, as discussed, can be one of reducing difference and enhancing what is shared.

Where children have individual characteristics that may make them vulnerable (and this would include SEND) you may need to make some modification to your approach in order to enable their contribution to the research process and facilitate the expression of their voices. This is another occasion on which it is enormously helpful to work with specialist staff in school who help support children in their day-to-day engagement with school. In Chapter 3, I discussed the use of photo-elicitation techniques to help with this for a participant, 'Jake'. Taking Jake's example, where using drawings and interviews in school with children aged 9 and 10yrs, the teaching assistant who worked with one of the children recognised the challenge that they would face in actively producing an image to use. Therefore, I worked with the class at a point where Jake was being given additional support on a one-to-one basis, so as not to visibly exclude him. Subsequently, the teaching assistant, being very familiar with Jake's home situation, was able to produce some photographs that we could use to structure his interview at a later time. This meant that Jake's participation was different but equivalent to his peers.

Jake's teaching assistant stayed with us during the interview and made an active contribution to our discussion of his experiences in play activities inside and outside of school – knowing how to most effectively communicate with him, she could support his engagement with prompts drawn from what she knew to be his experience, which he could then expand on, helping me understand his perspective. Such enrolling of support from staff is not something that we can expect as researchers and this was exceptional commitment by Jake's teaching assistant. But, if there is a willingness on behalf of the school and individuals involved, it is hugely helpful in ensuring voices are represented in education research.

Indeed, the focus of your research may in itself be to understand perspectives of vulnerable children, and such approaches will be crucial to ensure the safeguarding of those you are involving and the adequate representation of their voices. Further to such vulnerabilities as identified above, there will be the more nuanced, temporary social vulnerabilities that children may experience. Whilst these are not usually formally recognised, they can be informally recognisable and the intensity of some of the invisible 'vulnerabilities' that children may experience is very real.

This means that we are required to consider the social environments in which research is conducted. Ultimately, such attention needs to incorporate all phases of the research process, including the gaining of ethical approval, the production of visual data and the interpretation of that visual data through, for example, the use of interview (as discussed in Chapters 3 and 6).

When gaining ethical approval for projects, there is limited attention afforded to the subjective groupings of children in the research process. You will have had to consider the practicalities of how children are facilitated in electing not to participate and how you may assure anonymity and confidentiality, but the invisible power relations that exist between children is generally not accounted for in any explicit way here. It is, however, something that you do need to think about on a practical level. The shared decision-making that is taken in research that can reduce power differentials between researcher and researched are widely considered in discussion of creative approaches to research (Delph-Janiurek, 2001). However, there is a little less attention afforded to the power dynamics that can potentially exist between children, temporarily affecting their vulnerability.

In many instances, either for purely practical reasons or specific design purposes, when conducting research in school settings it is necessary and appropriate to work with children in groups or whole classes. The production of visual data in such contexts inevitably becomes a 'public' phenomenon. Even where the best efforts have been made to ask children to focus only on what they are doing, the reality is that they will look at one another's drawings and inevitably form opinions. Children dynamically negotiate their own power interrelations, which are frequently unequal (Lomax, 2012), and telling children to respect one another's efforts does not guarantee that they will (Audley & Jović, 2020). Therefore, whether opinions formed are expressed in front of you or not, they may be expressed to one another outside of the immediate environment, and this could be potentially negative in outcome. It is difficult to know whether this would have an impact on the particular children you are working with or what the outcomes may be, but be mindful of how children might interact to the disadvantage of some individuals, such as through ridicule by peers and through the sharing of their thoughts. As discussed in Chapter 4, children's voices are impacted by the hierarchies of cultural value that is placed on particular perspectives (Lomax, 2012).

One way of addressing this is to consider, where possible, conducting research either with individuals alone, or in pairs or small groups of their choice. I have found this particularly effective in primary school settings where the class is largely together for the day and (obviously with the teacher's agreement) can step outside to an area close by but removed where they can produce their artefacts. This is consistent with other researcher approaches (Burkitt, Watling, & Message, 2019) and has the advantage of removing them from the 'social gaze' that can objectify their work and open them to judgement, as discussed by Mannay et al. (2017). It enables you, perhaps, to create an environment that informally discusses the children's thought processes in what they are doing.

Thus, working with children as vulnerable participants, and vulnerable children within that group in school, has particular challenges as compared to other research environments. Such considerations are amplified when considering research subjects that may be considered 'sensitive' (Augusto & Hilário, 2019).

Researching sensitive subjects

Having borne in mind that all children are vulnerable participants, working with them on sensitive subjects can be a daunting prospect in terms of ensuring that they are both represented and protected within the processes of research. However, we are advised not to avoid this as important issues can be addressed on behalf of those who may not otherwise have their voices heard (Flanagan, 2012). There are conflicting views on what constitutes a sensitive topic in research and the use of the term has been criticised as lacking interrogation (Powell et al., 2018). However, where areas of investigation have been deemed to be 'sensitive' in educational research, it is considered to be that which is a potential threat to those who are involved in it, either from the perspective of researcher or participant. It is likely to involve some kind of disclosure of information or perspectives that would ordinarily remain private (Liamputtong, 2007).

Expanding on the 'threat' to you as researcher it is important to acknowledge that you may feel in a vulnerable position (Augusto & Hilário, 2019). If you are investigating a sensitive topic, you may in turn be affected by children's responses in a way that raises ethical issues. You therefore need to be confident enough, and have the appropriate support in place, to cope with such challenges. It is also of value to be aware that sometimes sensitivities arise from discussion within what had not been considered to be topics of particular sensitivity. Therefore, anticipating possibilities as far as you can will serve to mitigate against taking what may be an inappropriate response (Richardson, 2019).

Scenario

One of the ways of dealing with this is that, where there are concerns, alternative ways of approaching subjects can be considered. For example, one undergraduate student I was working with was interested in gender in school and, in particular, supporting transgender children in education. The student had wanted to use a phenomenological approach to his

> work and employ visual methods to understand the subjective experiences of such children. We therefore discussed the challenges of this and ethical concerns regarding whether the study was appropriate and justified. Ultimately, it was recognised that for the academic purposes of the work and the lack of potential positive outcome for the child, the study did not warrant being pursued. However, the topic was clearly of great emerging contemporary relevance and we therefore negotiated the pursuit of the topic but reframed the research question to problematise understanding the provision as experienced by the teachers and wider school. Taking this as an example – and related to discussions within this book that justify the use of visual methods in understanding children's perspectives – it may simply, in some cases, not be appropriate to do this.

Addressing sensitive topics means that children are perhaps more likely to disclose information that the researcher needs to share with other professionals in order to ensure safeguarding. This therefore means that you may feel disturbed by what the child is experiencing and that you need to make a judgement that negotiates the line between maintaining confidentiality and passing on information where a child may be vulnerable in a way that the school is not already aware of. Such discernments are very dependent upon experience and require a great deal of reflection on the suitability of addressing particular subjects in research. This really affects initial decisions as to whether a particular research question should be addressed in the first instance. If you are an experienced teacher conducting active research at master's level you are likely to be in a very different position to a novice researcher working on undergraduate study. Clearly, you will be given guidance on this from your supervisor in the first instance, and anticipating potential challenges needs to form part of your discussion.

The contested nature of 'empowerment'

Power can be seen to exist within the research process itself and the outcomes, in the sense of who benefits most from participating. The assumption here is that it is not fixed, owned or absolute but is rather a phenomenon that is negotiated and renegotiated in relationships (Foucault & Gordon, 1980).

The issue of assumed inequalities in power within research is highlighted by Swartz (2011), who emphasises the need to counter such imbalances in research endeavour. It was also a consideration highlighted to me very forcefully when I first began to conduct research with children. Presenting at a conference, I predicated my arguments on the fact that I was empowering children in the research process, thus validating the ethical justification of what I was doing and grounding my work (so I thought) on the laudable basis of facilitating children's expression. I therefore found that being abruptly challenged on this rather disrupted my sense of self-validation:

> How are you claiming that you're empowering children? Do they even care about what you're doing?
>
> (Conference delegate question)

What I was doing was giving children control over the research interaction but not understanding this in light of children actually benefiting from the research – being 'gifted' through it (Swartz, 2011). A more accurate description would be to identify that, particularly as an outsider to the school environment, I was the one who was benefiting (Swartz, 2011), and that the manipulation of power in the research process did enable a freer expression but that it was to my benefit rather than the children's directly.

There is a clear danger at this point that I am negating the work that I have done (and, indeed this text as a whole). The shift that has now taken place is that perhaps I argue with more considered appreciation as to the discourse that I use to frame the research that I do and/or that there is greater consideration as to the way in which children may benefit from taking part in any studies that I conduct. Therefore, where the contribution to the research process is being brought more closely within children's control, I would consider this to be 'agency in process'; where doing this leads ultimately to informed decisions that directly affect them, I would still claim a degree of empowerment. Essentially, the children are empowered to guide the process in constructing knowledge about themselves.

Foucault suggested personal knowledge is constructed through hierarchical observation, normalising judgement, and a combination of the two (Markula & Pringle, 2006). This theoretical basis can be used to explain what ordinarily happens within some institutional environments. What this approach is seeking to do is disrupt this pattern and work with children to redefine norms of engagement – to challenge elements of the research environment that might otherwise 'disempower' participants (Bracken-Roche, 2017).

In this sense, considering research context, we have a situation of the adult researcher being welcomed to the school by the key gatekeepers of the headteacher and teacher. Further permissions for participation in studies are then subject to subsequent consent of parents before coming to the children themselves. This potentially creates a hugely unequal environment in which we hope to productively work with children and claim we are interested in their expression of unhindered personal perspective. The challenge, therefore, is how to create environments that might redefine, or at least disrupt, children's perception of where power might lie.

Ball (2013, pp13–14) discusses the way that 'sinews of power' exist in everyday, mundane relationships. Using creative methods of research in which production of knowledge is led by children is a way of articulating, not simply through discourse, but action, that shared power in the research process, and thus challenging this perception (Mannay et al., 2017). This is central to the purposes of this research approach, as discussed in all other chapters within this text, and is perhaps the closest way that we can come to understand children's perspectives. Therefore, by managing relations, we can ensure that children feel empowered in the research process. Although you as a researcher are the one actually making the decisions as to how the research is designed, and within that exercising power, you are still ensuring that children's voices are heard in the construction of knowledge about them.

Empowerment in research as process

Thinking about the idea of empowerment as control forms a key argument that underpins the justification for using visual methods as research tools. In particular, this can form the essential basis of interaction between you as a researcher, your participants and the topic being addressed. On a most essential level, this concerns the process of interaction in data collection.

The research process that we are concerned with here is that which produces 'knowledge' – in this case, knowledge about children's experiences. Ordinarily, production of knowledge in school contexts is framed in the expectations of the school and in itself is a claim for power (Ball, 2013). Research approaches described here are a way of producing knowledge about children that is controlled by children. As I write I am mindful of my use of language as we see many examples of claims to, for example, 'give' children a voice. I acknowledge, therefore, that it is not really possible to adequately avoid any sense of hierarchy involved in the research process, but what can be created is a shift in the balance of control in an enabling sense (e.g. reducing the number of decisions made by the researcher and increasing those of the participant) that is then responded to in a reflective way. For example, the researcher actively considers the way in which they may be filtering the data in analytic processes they employ, seeking to identify and reduce the extent to which they may be affected by interpretive processes.

So, how does the production of creative artefacts support this power renegotiation? To begin with, you as the researcher will set the topic for investigation, but, from then on, the child is free to respond as they wish. Key ways in which this may be achieved in a 'creative methods' context would be:

a   Selection of tool (e.g. drawing, photograph, photo-voice)
b   Decision-making regarding content
c   Control of interview conversations

If we take the tool selection for the child – it may be, as discussed in Chapter 3, that you will select a tool for a specific purpose, and therefore this would not form part of the control that the child participants will take – participants making a selection here means that they can choose a way of expressing themselves that they feel most comfortable with and/or best able to manipulate as a means of communication, or that which they think they will have most fun using. Ideally, their

The nature of power and empowerment 81

Figure 5.2 Kyle's captioned picture submitted in lieu of his own drawing (aged 14yrs). Caption: This is how I feel if I try to draw (I'm the one in the middle!) (PS can we just chat?)

selection will address all three. In cases where children are not given choice, they can find ways of letting you know – an example is given in Figure 5.2, which shows a captioned picture Kyle brought in after having been asked to draw.

This picture, in practice, actually served well in establishing the basis for an interview with Kyle, as it brought humour to his contribution. It also indicates that it is not necessary to see children entirely as victims in terms of power differentials and that, with good relationships, they can feel very comfortable in letting you know their thoughts if they differ from yours.

This emphasises that, ultimately, an element of choice in what to produce and how to produce it gives an element of control and can set the context for your later discussion, which can be based on open questions inviting participants to tell you what they think.

Empowerment and ownership of interpretation

The interpretation of data is addressed in detail in Chapter 6, therefore, attention at this point will be drawn just to the considerations that you might need to make in terms of the way this affects power relations with your participants. The way in which you address this will, as with all other decisions that you make regarding your work with minors, depend on factors such as age, vulnerabilities and the individual circumstances of those that you're working with as regards to the school environment. But crucial to this process is a willingness to check what it is you are being told – visually or verbally – and avoid the temptation to start categorising information too early in the process.

Checking the validity of the interpretation of what any research participant is saying is crucial. This needs to be included at all stages of the research process and is likely to take the form of checking for understanding in two directions: firstly, that your participants have understood the question(s) that you are asking of them and, secondly, that you are understanding what they are telling you. I deliberately switch my tense use in this preceding sentence to emphasise the need for you, as a researcher, to continually check that you are understanding, as it is possible that the messages your participants want to convey actually change during the process. This may mean that you take a conventional approach to demonstrating a willingness to listen, as in the use of repeating information back to your participant. What I have found it also sometimes requires is an ability to take a silent note and then revisit the point at a later stage in your discussions. Throughout this process it is necessary to regard your participants, rather than yourself, as 'expert' (Gómez et al., 2019). In terms also of the final analysis that you engage in, it can be appropriate to work with children directly to do this, and this is discussed further in the following chapter.

Ethical considerations

Research with human subjects is generally ethically challenging, and research with children particularly so (Munro et al., 2005). Within this chapter (as generally within this text) there is an emphasis on building relationships with children, and this in itself can be regarded as an ethical strategy (Swartz, 2011) as you are building trust, ensuring understanding and assuring participants through evidencing your own investment in them. Dealing with some of the unexpected responses of children can present genuine dilemmas for researchers and, in some instances, you may have to consider your response on a moral as well as ethical basis. It is wise to pre-empt such possible challenges (Richardson, 2019).

Essentially, you will be creating conditions where children can exercise 'ethical agency' and express how they feel about being involved in all stages of your research (Mortari & Harcourt, 2012). Ethical issues are particularly enhanced when considering the concepts of power (Swartz, 2011) and, therefore, establishing relationships and taking approaches that reduce inequalities contributes to an ethical approach. Through the processes discussed above, you will be endeavouring to minimise distress with respect to addressing sensitive topics, either as part of your planned work or as they arise within your study.

The significance of ethical considerations is also further highlighted with respect to issues of power when exploring sensitive topics (Powell et al., 2018) and/or working with vulnerable children (in whichever ways they are vulnerable). A constant questioning of power roles within the dynamics of the relationships that you build with children, either individually and/or as groups, can address some of the tensions associated with this, even if it is not possible to fully mitigate against power differentials (Collier, 2019).

By their rationalised nature, creative researchers using creative approaches seek to reduce differentials in power relationships. As they generally involve a number of stages and a collaborative approach to the research topic, they generate opportune points at which, for example, informed consent/assent can be reaffirmed or renegotiated. Continued questioning of power roles in creative research necessarily identifies that there will not be a point at which differentials are eliminated or, indeed, secured at a minimal level in any finite sense. In recognising this, we do, however, establish a basis for what we can claim to be ethical research (Collier, 2019; Oulton et al., 2016).

A key factor when considering aspects of power relationships is the access that gatekeepers provide. You will need to gain permissions from parents but also be aware that some children will have guardians. There may be greater sensitivities associated with children who are looked after – again, seek advice from the class teacher to ensure that you are appropriately aware of children's situations. It is incumbent upon you as the researcher to ensure that the consent of gatekeepers does not necessarily transfer to assumed consent of children. By this, I do not refer simply to any formalised process that might be employed (such as in the signing of paperwork) but that there is a genuine attempt to ensure children understand what they are becoming involved with and are happy to be so (Arnott, Martinez-Lejarreta, Wall, Blaisdell, & Palaiologou, 2020). Here, it is important to attend to symbolic messaging as may be conveyed through children's behavioural characteristics, such as in body language during a project (Arnott et al., 2020; Slepičková & Bartošová, 2014). This may occur where children do not feel able to take up the opportunities to speak in safe places to tell you if they are uncomfortable with what they are doing. It is important that you attend to such responses, talk to the children and, if you are left in any doubt as to whether the child wishes to continue involvement, ensure that you do not use their data. You may be able to give the appearance externally that the child is still involved whilst ensuring that you do not include their data if you have evidence that the child does not really wish to continue to be so involved.

You could also include ways of children letting you know 'privately' whether they want to be involved or continue to be involved in your study. For example, if you have a whole class completing a drawing, each child could put a tick or a cross on the back of the image to indicate whether they want their picture to be used or not. It could also be helpful, if you have an appropriate environment in which to do this, to set up a 'suggestions box' for children to communicate ideas or concerns with you anonymously. In this way your attention to ethics will permeate your research as is advised (Chesworth, 2016; Flanagan, 2012).

A further key factor to be aware of is the potential for children to take up the values and orientations of the adults that have given permissions that may not have necessarily aligned with their own. This can lead to the reinforcement of power environments as existed prior to the research (Collier, 2019) and can limit the understanding of perspectives that you may be seeking.

Such considerations raise their own questions of hierarchies of power but, in this case, they exist in the relative status and authority of the different levels and domains of responsibility (Mortari & Harcourt, 2012). In this sense, your ability to renegotiate may be limited – if a headteacher does not give consent for work to be carried out in their school, then no further progress can be made. This highlights the need for you to be very clear when presenting the purposes of your research and your intentions as to how it might be carried out, and to the benefit of whom. The whole research process involves a complexity of relationships of those holding different forms of power that can affect the ethical processes that you engage in (Graham et al., 2012).

Related to this is the converse situation where some children may be prevented from participating in your study as a result of parents refusing to provide consent (Sendil & Sonmez, 2020). This is a challenging one as, if you have considered it to be important for parents/guardians to approve of their charge's involvement, then refusal to do so means that you cannot include the child in the study you are completing. In such cases, it is important to ensure that this does not give a complete sense of exclusion. An example of what this may look like in practice, if the topic is not considered to be sensitive, may be that the child can still produce an artefact but their product will not used in your analysis and they will not be involved in any further engagement such as interviews. If such an adaptation is not appropriate, then empathetic management of the situation through working with the teacher needs to be applied to the situation.

Such limitations may also be exacerbated by the environments in which your research is taking place, in the sense that schools, in a structural sense, are environments that locate children as individuals to be acted upon (Collier, 2019). Therefore, an awareness of this can help with the ethics of reducing power differentials in the sense of redefining space and its use, as discussed in Chapter 4.

Many research studies offer incentives to take part – when working with children the appropriateness of this can be questionable in any instance and, when addressing sensitive issues, particularly so. However, it is possible to offer these where it is 'commensurate with good sense, such that the level of incentive does not impinge on the free decision to participate' (BERA, 2018). Providing some kind of recognition for contribution can also be desirable, as children's efforts should be recognised. How you do this will depend on the school – some that I have worked with, for example, do not allow children to receive material rewards. Generally speaking, creating a certificate of recognition can work very effectively in ensuring that children feel that their contribution has been valued, particularly if they are of primary school age. This would therefore be more reward than incentive, which may well be more appropriate for children. In any instance, ethically, you are likely to need to ensure that you have not enticed children to take part in your study but do recognise participants' contribution.

As indicated above, if investigating more sensitive issues, it is also important to consider the impact that the research could have on you (Vaswani, 2018) and, just as you may refer children for additional support, you may need to be prepared yourself to seek this. Your approach will not only be navigating the need to prevent harm to children, with their right to be heard (Mudaly & Goddard, 2009), but also your desire to represent a particular set of experiences, and the impact the processes of doing so may have on you.

There is, of course, a degree of irony embedded in this discussion of ethics associated with concerns of power and empowerment, as many of the suggestions here place the onus on you as a researcher to create an environment that is supportive of your participants – therefore, you are necessarily exercising a form of power in the very act of doing this. Ultimately, discussions of reducing power differentials can only ever be intentional and will never be finite, but, nonetheless, are crucial to conducting research that can be considered ethical.

Conclusion

This chapter has considered what we mean by power and how it can be renegotiated within research with children. Generally speaking, in research, you are entering the field that is defined through uneven power distributions that you will need to address when considering your approach. If power is viewed as malleable and renegotiable, then you can work towards a sense of empowerment for your child participants. Investigating sensitive topics usually demands enhanced ethical considerations but do not mean that they cannot, or should not, be addressed. Similarly, when working with vulnerable children, there may be a requirement for more nuanced approaches to ways in which children may be empowered by your work. This section therefore summarises the need to address pre-existing assumptions regarding power relations in research in order to ensure authenticity in your work.

You should now have an understanding that:

As power operates within society, as you enter your research, you will be perceived to be in a power*ful* position relative to your participants

Power is not an absolute phenomenon and can be negotiated to ensure children feel free to express their perspectives

Issues of power are enhanced when working with particularly vulnerable participants and/or considering sensitive topics – however, all research involves an element of inequality that needs to be addressed

Having considered how we might influence power distribution in the research process, the following chapter addresses how data produced in these processes can be analysed. Consideration is given to the way that meaning in the artefacts produced by children may not always be immediately visible, and that data interpretation and analysis is an iterative, co-constructed process. It explores ensuring rigour in such processes and the ways in which it can, itself, be a creative exploration of meaning.

References

Arnott, L., Martinez-Lejarreta, L., Wall, K., Blaisdell, C., & Palaiologou, I. (2020). Reflecting on three creative approaches to informed consent with children under six. *British Educational Research Journal*, 46(4), 786–810. doi:10.1002/berj.3619.

Audley, S., & Jović, S. (2020). Making meaning of children's social interactions: the value tensions among school, classroom, and peer culture. *Learning, Culture and Social Interaction*, 24. doi:10.1016/j.lcsi.2019.100357.

Augusto, F. R., & Hilário, A. P. (2019). "Through the looking glass": the emotional journey of the volunteer ethnographer when researching sensitive topics with vulnerable populations. *The Qualitative Report*, 24(13), 17–30.

Ball, S. J. (2013). *Foucault, Power, and Education*. New York: Routledge.

BERA (2018). Ethical Guidelines for Educational Research, 4th ed.

Bracken-Roche, D., Bell, E., Macdonald, M. E., & Racine, E. (2017). The concept of 'vulnerability' in research ethics: an in-depth analysis of policies and guidelines. *Health Research Policy and Systems*, 15(1), 8. doi:10.1186/s12961-016-0164-6

Burkitt, E., Watling, D., & Message, H. (2019). Expressivity in children's drawings of themselves for adult audiences with varied authority and familiarity. *Journal of Developmental Psychology*, 37, 354–368.

Chesworth, L. (2016). A funds of knowledge approach to examining play interests: listening to children's and parents' perspectives. *International Journal of Early Years Education*, 24(3), 294–308. doi:10.1080/09669760.2016.1188370.

Collier, D. R. (2019). Re-imagining research partnerships: thinking through "co-research" and ethical practice with children and youth. *Studies in Social Justice*, 13(1), 40–58. doi:10.26522/ssj.v13i1.1926.

Cudworth, D. (2008). 'There is a little bit more than just delivering the stuff': policy, pedagogy and the education of Gypsy/Traveller children. *Critical Social Policy*, 28(3), 361.

Daniels, S. (2008). Physical education, school sport and Traveller children. *Physical Education Matters*, 3(3), 32–37.

Delph-Janiurek, T. (2001). (Un)consensual conversations: betweenness, 'material access', laughter and reflexivity in research. *Area*, 33(4), 414.

Flanagan, P. (2012). Ethical review and reflexivity in research of children's sexuality. *Sex Education*, 12(5), 535–544. doi:10.1080/14681811.2011.627731.

Foucault, M., & Gordon, C. (1980). *Power/Knowledge: Selected Interviews and Other Writings, 1972/1977*. Brighton: Harvester Press.

Freeman, M., & Mathison, S. (2008). *Researching Children's Experiences*. New York: Guilford Publications.

Gómez, A., Padrós, M., Ríos, O., Mara, L.-C., & Pukepuke, T. (2019). Reaching social impact through communicative methodology. Researching with rather than on vulnerable populations: the Roma case. *Frontiers in Education*, 4(9). doi:10.3389/feduc.2019.00009.

Gormally, S., & Coburn, A. (2014). Finding Nexus: connecting youth work and research practices. *British Educational Research Journal*, 40(5), 869–885. doi:10.1002/berj.3118.

Graham, A., Powell, M. A., & Taylor, N. (2015). Ethical research involving children. *Family Matters*, (96), 23–28.

Liamputtong, P. (2007). *Researching the Vulnerable: A Guide to Sensitive Research Methods*. London and Thousand Oaks, CA: SAGE.

Lomax, H. (2012). Contested voices? Methodological tensions in creative visual research with children. *International Journal of Social Research Methodology*, 15(2), 105–117. doi:10.1080/13645579.2012.649408.

Mannay, D., Staples, E., & Edwards, V. (2017). Visual methodologies, sand and psychoanalysis: employing creative participatory techniques to explore the educational experiences of mature students and children in care. *Visual Studies*, 32(4), 345–358. doi:10.1080/1472586X.2017.1363636.

Markula, P., & Pringle, R. (2006). *Foucault, Sport and Exercise: Power, Knowledge and Transforming the Self*. London: Routledge.

Mortari, L., & Harcourt, D. (2012). 'Living' ethical dilemmas for researchers when researching with children. *International Journal of Early Years Education*, 20(3), 234–243. doi:10.1080/09669760.2012.715409.

Mudaly, N., & Goddard, C. (2009). The ethics of involving children who have been abused in child abuse research. *International Journal of Children's Rights*, 17(2), 261–282.

Munro, E. R., Holmes, L., & Ward, H. (2005). Researching vulnerable groups: ethical issues and the effective conduct of research in local authorities. *The British Journal of Social Work*, 35(7), 1023–1038. doi:10.1093/bjsw/bch220.

Oulton, K., Gibson, F., Sell, D., Williams, A., Pratt, L., & Wray, J. (2016). Assent for children's participation in research: why it matters and making it meaningful. *Child: Care, Health & Development*, 42(4), 588–597. doi:10.1111/cch.12344.

Powell, M. A., McArthur, M., Chalmers, J., Graham, A., Moore, T., Spriggs, M., & Taplin, S. (2018). Sensitive topics in social research involving children. *International Journal of Social Research Methodology*, 21(6), 647–660. doi:10.1080/13645579.2018.1462882.

Richardson, T. (2019). 'Why haven't I got one of those?' A consideration regarding the need to protect non-participant children in early years research. *European Early Childhood Education Research Journal*, 27(1), 5–14. doi:10.1080/1350293X.2018.1556530.

Sendil, O., & Sonmez, S. (2020). Ethics in research including young children: views and experiences of researchers. *Ilkogretim Online*, 19(1), 87–99. doi:10.17051/ilkonline.2020.644821.

Slepičková, L., & Bartošová, M. K. (2014). Ethical and methodological associations in doing research on children in a school environment. *New Educational Review*, 38(4), 84–93.

Swartz, S. (2011). 'Going deep' and 'giving back': strategies for exceeding ethical expectations when researching amongst vulnerable youth. *Qualitative Research*, 11(1), 47–68. doi:10.1177/1468794110385885.

Vaswani, N. (2018). Learning from failure: are practitioner researchers the answer when conducting research on sensitive topics with vulnerable children and young people? *International Journal of Social Research Methodology*, 21(4), 499–512. doi:10.1080/13645579.2018.1434866.

Chapter 6

Interpretation and analysis

This chapter will consider how creative forms of data can be drawn together, interpreted and analysed. This will include reference to recognised forms of analysis of visual data and will explore the role that the researcher has had in the research process, and has in determining their own orientation to data interpretation.

Key discussion points will be:

- What we mean by interpretation and analysis
- Utilising researcher-recorded data (video, transcripts, field notes, observational data)
- Analysing data sets (using a dimensional model as a framework)
- Creative ways of analysing data
- Coding, categorising and theming
- The process as a whole
- Ethical considerations

What we mean by interpretation and analysis

Despite the growth in the use of creative data in research and, in particular, visual methods, attention as to how to approach analysis has been limited (Drew & Guillemin, 2014; Freeman & Mathison, 2008; Kara, 2015; Luttrell, 2010). Considering how to interpret data is a key element of preparation for your research so, although this chapter appears towards the end of this text, and, logically, it would seem that interpretation should actually occur after data collection has been completed, much work that utilises creative approaches in schools actually involves analysis throughout all stages of the research process.

Mann and Warr (2017) suggest that the process of analysis in creative approaches to research lacks articulation – this chapter seeks to offer a framework for how analysis may look throughout your project and guide you through some of the decision-making that you will need to engage in as part of this. To begin with, it may be of value to think about how you interpret data analysis:

> **Thinking points**
>
> What do you understand by the terms 'interpretation' and 'analysis'?
> At what point do you think you will begin to do these things?
> How might the decisions that you make in your research planning impact on your later analysis?

I would suggest that, essentially, the point from which you first begin to discuss conducting research in the school you are working with, is the point at which you begin to generate your own data regarding the context that will frame your study. Recording responses of 'the school' and individuals within it to your approach can help support later analysis and constructively inform the decisions that you make.

Each of the phases of research, which we can refer to as preparation, conducting the study and processing of data, incorporates an element of interpretation and analysis to varying degrees. For the purposes of this chapter, I will define interpretation as the process through which you may structure your understanding and analysis of creative evidence generated, endeavouring to ensure children's objectives can be 're'presented, maintaining the integrity of the original data (Dismore & Bailey, 2011; Everley & Macfadyen, 2019). Reflecting on the creative processes is inevitably fallible (Skains, 2018), and you therefore need to be constantly aware of the need to revisit what you think. It is paramount that what you show is consistent with the intentions of your participants (Culshaw, 2019; Rose, 2016).

In order to achieve an understanding of the school, if you are able to work with a class for any period of time it may be helpful to adopt an approach of 'slow listening' (Chesworth, 2016), which will inform your actions throughout your work and be an ongoing process that informs your interpretation. Taking time to assimilate the conversations that you hear around you in school over a period of time provides a way for you to create an understanding of the individuals and institutional practices that inevitably determine aspects of your analysis (Lipponen, Rajala, Hilppö, & Paananen, 2016).

This interpretation will also necessarily be subject to your own cultural understanding in relation to the research topic and associated experience (Mannay, Staples, & Edwards, 2017). This is, as discussed in Chapter 3, your 'positionality'. However, this is not a point of stasis, and finding out as much as possible about the school within which you are conducting your research, and the children you are working with, will help inform you about the environment and also help with your own interpretation of the culture you are seeing. Essentially, you will integrate what may be unfamiliar to you into your own interpretation and broaden your understanding as part of a hermeneutic (interpretive) process (Zimmerman, 2015).

Therefore, sensitising yourself to the environment through visiting the school/class prior to conducting the research in any formal way can help understand the socio-cultural contexts that you will be part of. This helps you when you come to establish a desirable temporary environment in which you will conduct your research. It also positively affects power relations by allowing your participants to get to know who you 'are' (as discussed in Chapter 5). This can help delimit the way in which interpretation can be in contradiction to the constructions of children, as can sometimes be the case in creative approaches (Lomax, 2012).

Although interpreting the research environment in the planning phase by integrating into the school where possible may not be a formal part of your work, as discussed in the earlier chapters of this book, making this an active process by taking notes and reflecting on these will assist with later analysis of data. Obviously, the extent to which you might be welcome to do this will depend on the particular school and class that you are engaging in your work, but the general rule is to take as many opportunities as possible to familiarise yourself within the field. If you are already embedded in the school then you are well positioned, as you will have a familiarity with the socio-cultural environment. If this is the case, then it may well be worth almost doing the opposite and stepping back from your role/context to try to ensure you really see what's there and how you might be contributing to it (this is discussed further in Chapter 7 as part of reflexive processes).

> **Scenario**
>
> *I think one of the hardest things when I was doing this was that I knew the kids already so it was a bit weird to then also ask them about what they thought of my subject – they enjoyed doing the photos and it worked well – I think it did anyway. I was really glad actually that I did the research with groups one after another rather than all at the same time as it helped me reflect a bit about what I thought I knew already ... it helped with the analysis. It also gave me a chance to talk to them about what I was doing and why – I think they thought it was a good idea to ... not exactly challenge what was happening ... but listening to children about what they thought of the extended school day that the head (headteacher) was trialling – the whole thing made them realise that we're a school community and really want to understand what's effective for everyone.*

The processes above could simply be carried out informally, however, it is helpful that you take this kind of familiarisation phase to analyse environments as you progress.

Utilising researcher-recorded data (video, transcripts, field notes, observational data)

This highlights the need to generate your own data to support your interpretation of the artefacts produced by children (as discussed in Chapter 4). As reinforced in much of this text, keeping field notes should be something that you do habitually for all research projects. On the most basic level this is keeping a record of events and action; however, if you can, it is well worth adding in some additional thoughts in a kind of meta-narrative around what you have previously recorded (Chapter 4 discusses this in more detail).

This works for me as it reduces the sense of linearity that sometimes appears in field notes that are purely chronological by serving to build depth to my records and begin the process of analysis. The best thing to do is just experiment with what is most effective for you. The most important thing is that you ensure you do this in some form so that you do not miss this as a learning opportunity.

This provides you with an awareness of the socio-cultural environment that frames the way that children are engaging in your research. It also contextualises how you may interact with children and analyse the data that they generate. The following section focuses on how you might approach this utilising the contextual analysis that you have already established, beginning with what we may term a data 'set'.

Analysing data sets

This section discusses analysis of the physical materials and verbal data that you will have generated in collaboration with your participants. Here, I set out a model that can guide you in asking questions that explore the meanings that children derive from their experiences and how they are representing them. This is the analysis of a data 'set'. Having discussed a range of tools that can be used to facilitate expression with children, and how you can ensure data is viable, this framework can be applied to all data sets that have been generated for each child. Here, a data 'set' (see Figure 6.1) is considered to be the creative artefact that the child produced, the internal narrative of the artefact

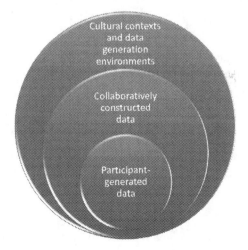

Figure 6.1 Data sets for children in school

Interpretation and analysis

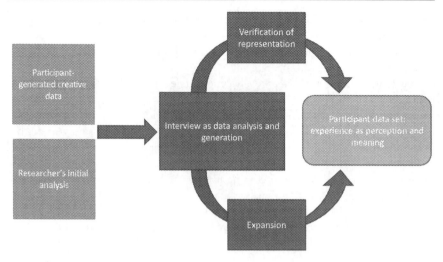

Figure 6.2 The process of generating your data set

(participant-produced data), the external narrative as co-constructed about the artefact and its meaning in relation to your research question (collaboratively constructed data), and the contextual information that you have been able to establish through observations and 'intelligent noticing' (cultural contexts and data generation environments) (Thomas, 1998, p151).

If we think about the processes through which you arrive at your data set, this can be operationalised using the diagram in Figure 6.2.

Within creative approaches to research, this data set is constituted by a repeated revisiting of data and inductive analysis. If we are to simplify this as a process, we have the participant-generated creative data and your own initial analysis based on your fieldwork and interaction with the child's artefact. You then generate a narrative (as discussed in Chapter 4) through which you analyse, by testing your interpretation through a process of verification and exploration of meaning through expansion. Ultimately, you have a data set that you can interrogate using processes of analysis. The considerations that you could make in order to do this in a systematic way that draws out meaning is modelled in Figure 6.3.

Figure 6.3 illustrates how children's data sets can be analysed. As a researcher it is important to consider the three dimensions of who/what is being presented, how this is being conveyed and why. This is a detailed and complex procedure. Such an approach can help interrogate the data that has been generated and create an understanding that is hermeneutically deep.

Who and what is being represented?

Potentially, the most logical point at which to begin your analysis of data is to look at who and what is there. Considering the 'who' of the content of your

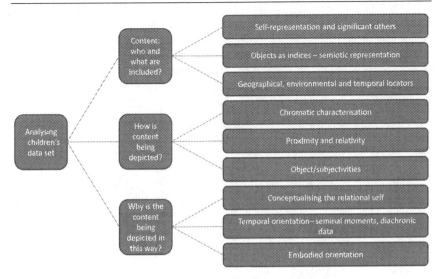

Figure 6.3 Dimensional model for analysis of children's data sets

participants' data, this demonstrates which individuals the children notice or recall about a particular situation. Identifying which individuals are included can inform you about the social context of the experience – as you build your data set it can also be significant to think about who could have been depicted but is not. You can also bear in mind that there may be people who are not directly referenced in an image but that may still exist in children's conceptualisation of what they have presented. For example, a photograph of the child's house may include to the child all who live in it, even though they are not visibly shown. Therefore, content in a data set may well be more than appears in the visual representation.

Mannay et al. (2017) described visual data as polysemic, in that there may be multiple inferences made from what is presented. It is, therefore, important to understand what is contained in the artefact produced by the children and also move beyond this (Everley, 2018; Freeman and Mathison, 2008). This is also because projective approaches to analysis frequently used with children's drawing that give weight to attributes such as size of representation of figures has been discredited if used in isolation (Burkitt, Watling, & Message, 2019; Schulze, 2017). It is also possible that data such as photographs illustrate representative and factual information simultaneously, and so this also needs to be accounted for (Drew & Guillemin, 2014). Therefore, you will have to have ensured that analysis is based on viable data by co-constructing an overview with your participants, which will have identified and addressed any points of intersemiotic divergence where meanings in what has been presented visually and verbally do not match (Hu & Qiu, 2019).

94 Interpretation and analysis

If considering the concept of relationships, you may also find that children will depict pets or representations of pets that can have a significant impact on how they perceive themselves. These can be incorporated into your data analysis in the same way as people, since they are generally accorded equivalent significance. Such references are likely to be given the status of 'who' rather than 'what'.

In terms of 'what' is included, this can indicate objects or environments that are important to the children. Some things to think about here include ideas that are objects to be acted on and also objects that contribute to the environment, or that fulfil both roles.

For example, a child depicting themselves with a bicycle, as in Figure 6.4 which shows part of Marisa's picture, may indicate a form of transport, a lifestyle activity or simply be there because it is a new acquisition of which the child is proud. There can also be points where features of artefacts are semiotic. For example, a group of children's artefacts may all feature themselves with a mobile phone, and this can identify where children have a shared focus that can be of cultural significance.

You may also be able to note some potential indexical links – these are features, for example, seen in photographs (Ledin & Machin, 2018), that are indicative of an emotional state (smiling), mood (cloud) or even the presence of something that is not immediately visible. For example, a photograph of an empty desk reminiscent of the child that would sit at it. In drawings, such strategies can be referred to as literal, where there is a direct correlation between what is presented and the associated emotion, as in the first example,

Figure 6.4 Marisa's picture of herself with her bike (aged 7yrs) (cropped image)

or non-literal where a device is used to project emotion, as in the second (Burkitt et al., 2019).

It can also be helpful to gain a sense of the temporal location of the data from indicators included in visual data and narratives. This could be in terms of the time of day (an after-school scene in a classroom has very different implications as compared to the same scene during curriculum time), time of year (a walk by the sea may mean something different in the summer as compared to the autumn) or frequency with which an event may take place (is it an occasional or recurrent event being depicted?)

This combines with geographical location. Where an event or events is/are taking place can be important in indicating the type of experience being expressed. Other environmental factors may also be identifiable such as rain/sunshine. These may represent actual physical conditions and may also be used to convey mood, as indicated above.

> **Thinking points**
>
> Consider the following analytical questions of content, 'Who and what':
>
> Who is being presented?
> Could there be individuals 'present' who are not visible?
> What purpose may the objects represented have?
> Are there semiotic representations being made?
> What features may be indexical links?
> What indicators of time can be identified?
> What indicators of geographical location are evident?

This now brings us to the question of in what way the content is being presented and the associated meaning that can be inferred from this.

How is content presented?

One factor in children's artefacts that will be immediately apparent is the chromatic representation, i.e. the colours that are utilised and the implications of this. Primary and bright colours are generally considered to have positive connotations, as will bright light in photographs. Conversely, secondary, darker colours or muted light will have negative associations. This creates a characterisation of mood that can inform you as to the creator's intentions.

Consideration of the relative orientation and proximity of different features within the artefact can inform you of relationships between characters or objects (see Figure 6.5), and can also indicate how participants are anticipating their audience. If figures are distant from one another it could give a sense of tension in relationships; if positioned close together, the opposite. The same

96 Interpretation and analysis

Figure 6.5 Representation of friendship (Michael, aged 14yrs)

can apply for other objects that may seem within or outside of 'reach'. Angles of representation, particularly in photographs, can further indicate relationships, for example, with an orientation looking down positioning the viewer in a position of power; oblique angles can be indicative of playfulness or tension (Ledin & Machin, 2018).

Considering the representation in Figure 6.5, there is clear use of light and dark that is contextualising the meaning that Michael is conveying here. The figures are also represented from an angle that indicates relative power, and their proximity to one another, unity. This was an image that was selected by Michael rather than being taken for the purposes of the research in the first instance. Therefore, the audience was not the researcher and original purpose not the research. The concepts of who is being represented here, and for what purposes, would present the basis of the analysis here.

If we return to Marisa's picture, Figure 6.6 represents the full image that she drew.

Considering this thinking about proximity only, she is looking directly at the audience rather than the other characters in the image. The other characters are placed behind her, and appear to be watching her, making her the focus of their attention. There are potential indexical links between representations of sunshine and positive mood.

Related to this are questions of objectivity and subjectivity. Within the data analysis model here, this operates on three levels. In one sense, this concerns focus on which elements form part of the intended action and message of the data

Interpretation and analysis 97

Figure 6.6 Marisa's full picture (aged 7yrs)

(subjectivity) and which are those elements being acted upon (objectivity). Additionally, the child may be present themselves as the object of an action (e.g. the child being taught) or as subject (e.g. the child learning). This also includes consideration of what aspects of the data are intended to generate a response in the observer (subjectivity) and which are intended to be observed only (objectivity). It is worth bearing in mind here that this may well be affected by the way in which the original task was set and who the child believes will be the audience for their data (Burkitt et al., 2019).

> **Thinking points**
>
> Analytical questions of *how* content is depicted:
>
> What colours are being utilised?
> What light/darkness is evident?
> How are objects being presented in terms of proximity to each other?
> How are you being invited to engage with the data as its audience?

98　Interpretation and analysis

Why is content presented as it is?

This leads to consideration of how children are presenting themselves in terms of understanding what their sense of 'self' within the topic of concern looks like. It also concerns how this self exists relationally with reference to other characters and, indeed, in relation to the subject being investigated. In our model, this is referred to as the 'relational self' and conceptualises how children see who they are with respect to how they are presenting their response to the research topic.

The permanency, or otherwise, of this self can be indicated by identifying the temporal location of your data (when things have occurred). This is helpful in seeking an understanding on the most basic level of when event(s) took (or are taking) place but, also, the potential transitory or more enduring nature of the experience the child is describing. This can also help expose which events may have been seminal in affecting children's orientation to the topic being investigated, have a long-term effect, or which may generate diachronic data that serves to give an historic context to children's perceptions by indicating how these have evolved over time.

In turn, this may affect children's embodied orientation in terms of how they physically experience particular events. If we think back to the example of Jeremy's presentation of himself in school (Chapter 3), his clay model was indicative of reducing his physical presence as much as possible, so as not to be noticed. This emanated from experiences at home where he had felt the need to learn to hide from a particular adult when they were in the house. Therefore, previous experiences can be seen to inform action, and this action can be transferred from one environment to another.

> **Thinking points**
>
> Analytic questions to understand *why* children have presented experience in a particular way:
>
> Where does the child see themself in this experience?
> What is the relationship between the child and other characters in the experience?
> How has this experience affected the child?
> Has this effect been transitory or more lasting?

If we can combine the answers to the questions above, we can gain an understanding of children's experience and establish a representation of perceptions and meanings. These can then be turned into data to answer your research question and begin to predict the change that needs to take place in order to optimise children's projected experiences.

A further thought in terms of what may be helpful, even when ensuring that you speak to children about their artefacts, is to take care not to make assumptions:

Scenario

In one particular instance a boy drew me a picture of his family at home – there were five members of the family standing facing forward and a third apparently floating above them. In my preparations to speak to him I became very conscious that this could represent the loss of a family member and that perhaps the additional figure was, for example, 'in heaven'. Following some introductory exchanges, the conversation turned to Eliot's drawing and continued as follows:

SUZANNE: So ... thank you for doing this drawing – it looks really interesting – can you explain it to me?

ELIOT: Yep; this is my mum and my dad and my uncle (pointing to the three standing figures on the left) (pause ...) and these two are my brothers (pointing to the remaining standing figures and saying their names), and this is my other brother, Isaac (pointing to the floating figure), ... we're in the park near our house.

SUZANNE: And I see you've drawn most of your family here, and Isaac here ... can you tell me why you wanted to do this? (preparing to deal with a sensitive situation).

ELIOT: Well I would of done him here (indicating next to the rest of the family) but it wouldn't fit so I done him there instead ... (Eliot, aged 6yrs).

Essentially, what you will be doing is attending to both internal and external narratives of the data and therein enhancing the analytical scope of your work (Freeman & Mathison, 2008).

One factor that it is of value to think about when seeking assurances that represented meanings are children's own, is to use your observations and interactions to seek to verify that children are conveying personal perspectives rather than adopting a visualised equivalent of ventriloquation, wherein the words of others are used to create meaning (Luttrell, 2010). This is a particular concern where there is a mismatch between aspects of data generated. An example of this can be seen in Ellie's diary entry:

> You need to eat good things like fruit and vegetables. That's what I always eat.

And, when subsequently discussing the research topic:

> We mostly have noodles, I like noodles – those curry ones in the yellow pot.

Therefore, these two forms of communication need to be reconciled between what may appear to be the child saying what is expected to representing the child's actual understanding and perception. At the risk of imposing adult interpretation, it would appear here that the child knows what 'should' be healthy and therefore tell us this, but that it does not actually form part of the child's practice. This brings us to understanding the development of an overall narrative that explains experience and makes our conclusions manageable. Some of the ways in which this may be completed include creative ways of processing and summarising your analysis.

Creative ways of analysing data

Creating a narrative to represent an overview of your data can then be used to analyse your findings. This creates representation in storied form and can be helpful in drawing together heterogenous data – it can be especially useful if you have given children a choice of which creative tool to use in their approach, as it draws evidence together in a single, manageable form.

It is also possible to consider using other creative ways of analysing data. This approach can take a variety of forms and can be reflective of the creative approach that you consider most suited to your data collection. The following section explores a number of ways in which authors have approached this – these serve as suggestions but could be extended beyond the practical tools identified here, particularly if you have specific expertise/interests that you can employ for analytic purposes.

Mann and Warr (2017) explored the use of montage as 'representational practice' that can help in the analysis of complex data. Essentially, a physical pinboard of key outcomes of the research is created that enables the researcher to stand back and view what may separately appear as disparate phenomena – this can enable relationships between key points to be identified. This process can acknowledge the non-linear nature of experience and context, and help investigate what shared meanings may exist within the mass of data that has been created, whilst acknowledging there is no single 'truth'.

Other authors have suggested it is appropriate to reflect the specific tools that were used by participants within your analysis, where your own expertise is sufficient to do so. McCaffrey and Edwards (2015) discussed research that had been conducted in music education being processed through writing a song, which enabled the inclusion of contextual information that they suggest can be missed through more conventional means of data analysis. Similarly, Kara (2015) has also outlined suggestions of producing poetry to help analyse narrative data.

Perhaps avoiding the need for specific artistic/linguistic abilities is the recommendation by Buckley and Waring (2013) that diagramming is an underused but effective way of analysing data. This can create alternative ways of seeing information and help with theorising data. Computer-generated mapping can also be used, although simply drawing out graphics by hand is useful too and can help invite critical comment, for example from colleagues, supervisors or participants themselves, as it makes your thought processes readily accessible. Although these authors focus their work specifically on grounding theory, sensitising concepts from existing theoretical perspectives can be incorporated. It is also an approach that can be used throughout your work to visually hypothesise as you progress. Generating theory in creative ways combines inductive and deductive thinking to develop and test theory (Konecki, 2019).

Coding, categorising and theming

What you will have generated in your work with children to produce original data, and in associated interviews, is the potential to create an overview of each child's experience. From this process you can generate a narrative or creative product, as described above, that can then be analysed by identifying categories or themes that address your research question. Considering your research topic, you will have been coding your data by indexing key points. What needs to happen next will be determined by the nature of your research question and the original aims of your work, as there are many ways to analyse data (Kara, 2015).

If you are completing phenomenographic research you will be assuming that there are a limited number of ways in which children will be experiencing your focus of investigation (this is usually between two and six). These you can categorise by grouping the data (Larsson & Holmstrom, 2007; Tight, 2016). Here you will be identifying how children have engaged intentionally with the phenomenon that you are concerned with (e.g. child-centred learning approaches) and created meaning around it. This will be informed by the way you will have framed your questions in your research design. Phenomenographic studies often stop at this stage as a descriptive representation. An example of a category might be 'decision-making in learning', which could incorporate group tasks, teacher guidance, activity choice, etc. If you are utilising a specific theoretical perspective, you can use sensitising concepts from that theory as 'analytic categories' to understand the data (Freeman & Mathison, 2008; Kara, 2015). Alternatively, in order to maintain the sense of children's voices, retaining language as used by participants to name your codes is an effective way of categorising information (Giguere, 2011).

However, it may be appropriate to progress to identify themes that work within the data for a child, or across children's accounts. Clark and Braun created a six-stage model that is helpful for this from the discipline of psychology (Braun & Clarke, 2006). The first stage, familiarising yourself with the data, and the second, generating codes, you will have done in the process above. You would then revisit your coding and search for themes within this, and then revisit again to check these themes make sense in light of the data before defining and naming them (stages 3–5). The final stage is the writing up of your findings in your report or thesis. Within my work, an example of themes in what children value in physical activity were those of social engagement and social identity (Everley & Macfadyen, 2019) – these were concepts prioritised as meaningful to children and that informed their behaviours. Giguere (2011) refers to this as finding moments of meaning as phenomenological instances informing us about children's experiences. These themes need to be revisited within a process of critical reflexivity (Fletcher, 2013) where you question yourself and your assumptions (see Chapter 7 for a more detailed exploration of what this involves).

Further advice regarding the analysis of your data can be to take a step back from the data once it is collected to give yourself some space to incubate your thoughts (Hammershoj, 2014), or plan to include repeated times at which you do this where you create spaces to reflect (Nind & Vinha, 2016). This can help you 'see' the data more clearly and informally question your conclusions, as you can focus closely on key points and then look at the wider picture; a kind of zooming in and out of the research problem in light of the data.

A number of authors raise the question of the need to ensure that, as a researcher, you represent the voices of children authentically (Bailey, 2005; Luttrell, 2010). As has been discussed throughout this text, creative approaches to research usually represent an endeavour to understand and convey children's perspectives. If guidance in doing this is followed, then we can be confident that this is being achieved and that our coding, categorisation and theming is as it should be. However, a final consideration is whether to work with children in the analysis stages of the research to verify findings. Some authors suggest that it is appropriate to invite children to interpret data (Lipponen et al., 2016), or even allocate editorial rights to them (Luttrell, 2010) as regards to their own contribution. This ensures you have not only understood their intention but also that you are presenting them as they wish you to. It does, however, have practical implications in terms of needing to return to your participants at a number of points, so this possibly works best where you have a relatively small number of children that you are working with. It also has implications for wider understanding of your academically based investigation and, therefore, although we are situating children as experts in their own experience, it may not be appropriate to involve them in the application of their meaning.

Thus, the revisiting of your analysis once it's completed can be done in this way if appropriate. Working with another researcher can also be useful in this process, or even with teaching staff if they have an interest in your work. This was an approach that I used in one primary school when working with children of ages 5–6yrs when I generated a narrative based on a picture drawn, associated interview and additional information provided by their class teacher. On completion, we worked together to ensure that the brief narrative appeared authentic to the child's experiences. Alternatively, if you are a student, working with a peer using similar methods or investigating a similar topic can be helpful.

The process as a whole

Bringing all aspects of the research analysis process together, Figure 6.7 illustrates the stages that can be followed in generating your data set and then analysing this (bearing in mind that, as identified above, analysis will inevitably inform the research process as a whole at every stage). What we can see here is

Interpretation and analysis 103

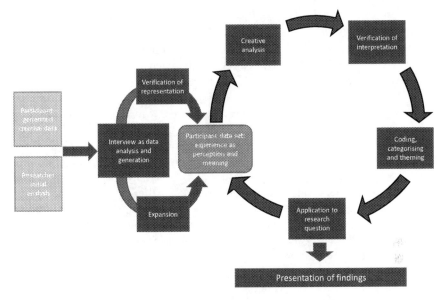

Figure 6.7 An overview of the analytic and interpretive processes

that once you have a data set, you can then analyse this creatively and verify your interpretation of this, either with participants, colleagues or both. Once you are satisfied that you are progressing appropriately you can move on to coding, categorising and theming your findings. Here it is helpful to acknowledge that you can move between stages (e.g. going back to revisit your creative analysis and the data set if you are not able to verify elements of your interpretation).

As you begin to draw your conclusions from the coding processes, you can then check that you have adequately addressed your research question, before revisiting the data or considering how you will present your findings and 'exit' this loop (see Figure 6.7).

Once you reach this stage, it is necessary to consider how you are ultimately representing your participants, and this is linked to ethical considerations that you may make.

Ethical considerations

Ensuring this process is ethically sound is, to some extent, a question of phronesis – thinking intelligently and morally in the process of discernment of what can be concluded from the data that children have generated. It underpins ensuring authenticity at the three sites where meaning is made around the child's visual artefact – the process of making it, what it means and how it is then seen (Culshaw, 2019). Ultimately, it is the navigation of a fine line in representing your participants and adequately interrogating the topic that you are investigating (Luttrell, 2010).

What is important also, is that you endeavour to present your interpretations in a way that is reflective of meaning – detailing accurately, as once the work has been submitted or published you will have little, if any, control over how it is interpreted (Aldridge, 2012). This not only depends on what you say, but also concerns your selection of images to represent your findings, which need to maintain the intended meaning of its creator.

Aligned to this are the considerations you may make with respect to the use of pseudonyms, as you will always need to protect the privacy of your participants (Brown, Spiro, & Quinton, 2020). Generally speaking, I will tend to use names (rather than numbers or similar) as I think it makes a final text feel more 'alive'. This does, however, raise the question of whether these should be culturally aligned with the background of your participants. Ideally, this would be the case, particularly where it has relevance to what you are discussing. However, some care needs to be taken in declaring this, as there are many names that have crossed cultures and it could be somewhat disingenuous and stereotyping to take this stance.

Also, in relation to the point of protecting identity, is the need to ensure that no unique aspects of children's experiences that could link statements to individuals are discussed in your work. This, therefore, represents the balance that you will need to achieve between representing children's voices authentically, as you are required to do (Hammersley, 2015), and ensuring anonymity in your work.

A final point on the same note is the representation of, and through, language. Swartz (2011) suggests that if an individual is communicating with young people in a language additional to their first, it may be appropriate to alter particular words when representing them, so that they do not appear inappropriately unsophisticated. On a personal level, I would quote verbatim in association with children's explanations of their artefacts but would ensure the cultural contexts in which the research is taking place are acknowledged. There is no 'right' or 'wrong' here, but there is a need to rationalise the choices that you make to ensure that what you represent has been thoughtfully and ethically justified.

Conclusion

This chapter has considered ways of interpreting data and approaching analysis. What is important here is that you incorporate data generated not only by your participants but your own data as evidenced through your observational note taking. This provides aspects of context to support your interpretation, involving a sense of space, place and relationships that affect the research environment. In turn, this interpretation needs to be verified and validated through interactions with your participants to ensure authenticity. There is a need to analyse the artefacts produced by children in their own right and relate this to narratives generated around these.

You should now have an understanding that:

Artefacts produced by children will often be saying more than is directly visible in their content
A process of verification within your analysis ensures integrity in your interpretation
Analysis is a process that forms part of the entire approach to your research, and your own observations and discussion with children forms an integral part of generating a data set for your participants
Analysis can incorporate creative approaches that are detailed and comprehensive

To ensure security in your findings and their representation, the need to be reflective and reflexive in what you are doing will underpin the interpretation and analysis activities that you engage in (Fletcher, 2013). These factors will be based on the investment that you have made in understanding your subjects, their environment and your own sense of self in relation to your study. The following chapter further considers how you might become sensitised to the research environment and maintain a sense of critical reflexivity. It considers how engaging in sensitising processes can enhance your understanding and empathy in research. It also addresses the nature of reflexivity and explores the impact that you, and your sense of who you are and how you interact with the research question and environment, can have on the approaches that you employ, analysing the effect that this has on your interpretive processes. It ultimately identifies the crucial nature of reflection and reflexion in ensuring ethically sound research.

References

Aldridge, J. (2012). The participation of vulnerable children in photographic research. *Visual Studies*, 27(1), 48–58. doi:10.1080/1472586X.2012.642957.

Bailey, R. (2005). Evaluating the relationship between physical education, sport and social inclusion. *Educational Review*, 57(1), 71–90. doi:10.1080/0013191042000274196.

Braun, V., & Clarke, V. (2006). Using thematic analysis in psychology. *Qualitative Research in Psychology*, 3(2), 77–101.

Brown, C., Spiro, J., & Quinton, S. (2020). The role of research ethics committees: friend or foe in educational research? An exploratory study. *British Educational Research Journal*, 46(4), 747–769. doi:10.1002/berj.3654.

Buckley, C. A., & Waring, M. J. (2013). Using diagrams to support the research process: examples from grounded theory. *Qualitative Research*, 13(2), 148–172.

Burkitt, E., Watling, D., & Message, H. (2019). Expressivity in children's drawings of themselves for adult audiences with varied authority and familiarity. *British Journal of Developmental Psychology*, 37(3), 354–368. doi:10.1111/bjdp.12278.

Chesworth, L. (2016). A funds of knowledge approach to examining play interests: listening to children's and parents' perspectives. *International Journal of Early Years Education*, 24(3), 294–308. doi:10.1080/09669760.2016.1188370.

Culshaw, S. (2019). The unspoken power of collage? Using an innovative arts-based research method to explore the experience of struggling as a teacher. *London Review of Education*, 17(3), 268–283. doi:10.18546/LRE.17.3.03.

Dismore, H., & Bailey, R. (2011). Fun and enjoyment in physical education: young people's attitudes. *Research Papers in Education*, 26(4), 499–516. doi:10.1080/02671522.2010.484866

Drew, S., & Guillemin, M. (2014). From photographs to findings: visual meaning-making and interpretive engagement in the analysis of participant-generated images. *Visual Studies*, 29(1), 54–67. doi:10.1080/1472586X.2014.862994.

Everley, S. (2018). Using visual research tools when working with children in a primary school setting. In R. Medcalfe & C. Mackintosh (Ed.), *Researching Difference in Sport and Physical Activity* (pp. 55–70). London and New York: Routledge.

Everley, S., & Macfadyen, T. (2019). "I like playing on my trampoline; it makes me feel alive." Valuing physical activity: perceptions and meanings for children and. *Education 3–13. International Journal of Primary, Elementary and Early Years Education*, 45(2), 151–175.

Fletcher, G. (2013). Of baby ducklings and clay pots: method and metaphor in HIV prevention, *Qualitative Health Research*, 23(11), 1551–1562.

Freeman, M., & Mathison, S. (2008). *Researching Children's Experiences*. New York: Guilford Publications.

Giguere, M. (2011). Social influences on the creative process: an examination of children's creativity and learning in dance. *International Journal of Education & the Arts*, 12(1.5), 1–13.

Hammershoj, L. G. (2014). Creativity in education as a question of cultivating sensuous forces. *Thinking Skills and Creativity*, 13, 168–182. doi:10.1016/j.tsc.2014.05.003.

Hammersley, M. (2015). Research ethics and the concept of children's rights. *Children & Society*, 29(6), 569–582. doi:10.1111/chso.12077.

Hu, Y., & Qiu, Q. (2019). A social semiotic approach to the attitudinal meanings in multimodal texts. *Theory and Practice in Language Studies*, 9(9), 1160–1166. doi:10.17507/tpls.0909.12

Kara, H. (2015). *Creative Research Methods in the Social Sciences – A Practical Guide*. Bristol: Policy Press.

Konecki, K. T. (2019). Creative thinking in qualitative research and analysis. *Qualitative Sociology Review*, 15(3), 6–25. doi:10.18778/1733-8077.15.3.01.

Larsson, J., & Holmstrom, I. (2007). 'Phenomenographic or phenomenological analysis: does it matter? Examples from a study on aneastheologists' work'. *International Journal of Qualitative Studies on Health and Well-Being*, 2(1), 55–64.

Ledin, P., & Machin, D. (2018). *Doing Visual Analysis: From Theory to Practice*. London: Sage.

Lipponen, L., Rajala, A., Hilppö, J., & Paananen, M. (2016). Exploring the foundations of visual methods used in research with children. *European Early Childhood Education Research Journal*, 24(6), 936–946. doi:10.1080/1350293X.2015.1062663.

Lomax, H. (2012). Contested voices? Methodological tensions in creative visual research with children. *International Journal of Social Research Methodology*, 15(2), 105–117. doi:10.1080/13645579.2012.649408.

Luttrell, W. (2010). 'A camera is a big responsibility': a lens for analysing children's visual voices. *Visual Studies*, 25(3), 224–237. doi:10.1080/1472586X.2010.523274.

Mann, R., & Warr, D. (2017). Using metaphor and montage to analyse and synthesise diverse qualitative data: exploring the local worlds of 'early school leavers'.

International Journal of Social Research Methodology, 20(6), 547–558. doi:10.1080/13645579.2016.1242316

Mannay, D., Staples, E., & Edwards, V. (2017). Visual methodologies, sand and psychoanalysis: employing creative participatory techniques to explore the educational experiences of mature students and children in care. *Visual Studies*, 32(4), 345–358. doi:10.1080/1472586X.2017.1363636.

McCaffrey, T., & Edwards, J. (2015). Meeting art with art: arts-based methods enhance researcher reflexivity in research with mental health service users. *Journal of Music Therapy*, 52(4), 515–532. doi:10.1093/jmt/thv016

Nind, M., & Vinha, H. (2016). Creative interactions with data: using visual and metaphorical devices in repeated focus groups. *Qualitative Research*, 16(1), 9.

Rose, G. (2016). *Visual Methodologies: An introduction to Researching with Visual Materials*, 4th Ed. London: SAGE Publications.

Schulze, S. (2017). The value of two modes of graphic elicitation interviews to explore factors that impact on student learning in higher education. *Qualitative Sociology Review*, 13(2), 60–77.

Skains, R. L. (2018). Creative practice as research: discourse on methodology. *Media Practice & Education*, 19(1), 82–97. doi:10.1080/14682753.2017.1362175.

Swartz, S. (2011). 'Going deep' and 'giving back': strategies for exceeding ethical expectations when researching amongst vulnerable youth. *Qualitative Research*, 11(1), 47–68. doi:10.1177/1468794110385885.

Thomas, G. (1998). The myth of rational research. *British Educational Research Journal*, 24(2), 141–162.

Tight, M. (2016). Phenomenography: the development and application of an innovative research design in higher education research. *International Journal of Social Research Methodology*, 19(3), 319–338. doi:10.1080/13645579.2015.1010284.

Zimmerman, J. (2015). *Hermeneutics – A Very Short Introduction*. Oxford: Oxford University Press.

Chapter 7

Research sensitivities and reflections

This chapter addresses the nature of conducting research with children and young people from the perspective of the concerns of the researcher as a creative, reflective practitioner, as well as their vulnerabilities in research environments. Attention will focus on issues directly associated with topics of investigation and subjects, and also unanticipated disclosures that may arise through children and young people's interactions in these contexts.

Throughout this text I have argued for the place of creative approaches to research as an effective and appropriate means to explore subjective experiences of children. This has been set in the context that it is most complex where the research design, implementation and analysis involve thinking creatively in some way. Chapter 5 discussed being sensitive to your research relationships with children and young people that you may be working with, and forms one of the most important elements of your research approach. This concluding chapter will address your own orientation to your work and considers ways of sensitising yourself to the research.

Key discussion points will be:

- Sensitisation to research tools
- Purposes of reflection and reflexion in the research process
- The practicalities of reflection and reflexion
- The axiology of research tool selection
- Ethical considerations

Sensitisation to research tools

Although we have established an argument supporting the selection of what may be used as a research tool within creative research on the basis of theorised efficacy, it is also worth considering how we can establish an understanding of how this might 'feel' to participants. This has been acknowledged in earlier chapters, but I return to the point here as establishing some kind of empathy with the approaches yourself could enhance your understanding of how they function in practice. Kara (2015) argues that as a researcher, if using drawings, you should be competent in drawing. If we consider some researchers who have utilised drawings, we can indeed identify such levels of competence. Hannah Gravestock is an example of one such researcher. As an author she has used drawings in research exploring sport – she is a hugely accomplished figure skater and artist with her website entitled 'Draw/Perform/Research' (http://hannah-gravestock.co.uk/read-watched-and-heard/). Hannah does not specifically work with children, however, and utilises drawings as performance, so this creates a different context and usage to visual research. Taking Kara's point though, it is difficult to imagine anyone more 'qualified' to explore the topic that she focuses her research on using the tools that she does, and she is genuinely inspirational because of this. I would, however, suggest that having a level of competence in 'art' is not a prerequisite and, in fact, could even be detrimental to your work in a school context, particularly if children are concerned with the possibility that they will be judged on artistic merit.

Nevertheless, in terms of developing skills of empathy with how you might be asking your participants to engage with the research question, it is of great benefit to give yourself the task of responding as you would through the tools that you are asking your participants to use. The way in which you do this may well depend on what your research question is. You may be able to respond directly to the issue being addressed or need to adapt it so that it is appropriate for you. For example, I would not be able to make a representation of what it is to be a child of BAME background in a predominantly white school within the UK, but I could think about what it is to be an ethnic minority as a teacher, having worked in Japanese state schools. Responding to your own adapted research question using the methods and tools you envisage employing in your work can help develop empathy for your selected research tool and sensitise yourself to what you are doing (Culshaw, 2019). This can also have a very practical application as, particularly if you are utilising a novel approach (either to you or your participants), it can avoid some of the pitfalls that you may find where the tool is not as useful as you first thought (see Chapter 3 for a discussion of different approaches).

Understanding the tools that you are using forms an essential part of creative approaches to research, and sensitisation to these informs both the nuances and practicalities of your selected research design. Engaging in a creative 'act' could support the type of divergent thinking that was explored in Chapter 2, as recommended by Fautley and Savage (2007). Thinking purposefully in this process will support the application of an imaginative approach that can underpin creativity (Hammershoj, 2014). This therefore establishes a point of departure that potentially characterises your research throughout. This also ensures a depth of consciousness within the decision-making that you engage with in your research. It incorporates concepts of both 'reflection' and 'reflexion' as essential factors in ensuring the quality of your work, and these will be discussed in the following section.

Purposes of reflection and reflexion in the research process

Traditional approaches to research have often advocated the adoption of a value-neutral approach that purportedly ensures objectivity (Greenbank, 2003; Kara, 2015). This intention has been evident in the selection of what is valued as a research topic, the tools that are used to investigate this and the ways in which data is analysed. However, as identified earlier in this text, research conducted with children that acknowledges the need to explore subjectivities and requires a more complex approach that is based on relationships fundamentally challenges the concept of objectivity. What is required is an active engagement through the kind of 'intelligent noticing' (Thomas, 1998) discussed in the preceding chapter. This, in turn, demands the ability to step back and ensure that you question what it is you are noticing and why. In order to ensure that research does not simply reinforce pre-existing expectations by applying some kind of personalised or theoretically skewed filter (Konecki, 2019), it is necessary to establish such a reflexive stance (Fletcher, 2013; Lynch, 2008; Warburton, 2016).

Beginning, however, with the concept of reflection, if you are involved in education as a teacher or are training to be a teacher, reflective practice is likely to be embedded into your professional work/training (Everley and Flemons, 2020). Such an approach equally applies to operating within schools as a research context. Reflecting on your research through, for example, noting what is going on in the school environment and the impact that this has on your data collection, can provide valuable information for use in data analysis, as discussed in Chapter 6. The extract below is an example of reflective notes made during an observation period within a high school context, which took place alongside the collection of data through children's journaling. The first comment refers to observation notes taken during the lesson (children aged 15 and 16yrs), which formed the basis of later reflections:

> Basketball Year 11 Miss Blackwood (Week A) Some of rounders group joined with usual basketball group. New arrivals dominated group with 'consent' of existing players; appear more able than usual group; seems to be respected. Penny hardly featured – usually 'key' player tendency to run up and down court without receiving ball. Penny receiving ball and not playing for a layup as usual – seems very excluded from the game.
>
> Ball passed so hard to Carrie three times in a row that she could not possibly have caught it (neither probably could have throwers). This was followed by complaints to her. Ended up in tears at side at end of particular game and then did not join in when her team played again. Eventually joined another team in order to take part. No notable difference in Clive's playing. Bridie played well under these conditions. Others continued attempts – esp. Nicola – great deal of application.

I then returned to these notes after school to reflect on what my observations might mean for my research, which was focusing on children's experiences of physical education:

> The change in group dynamics of the class appears to be significantly impacting on what some of the young people are achieving – seems to be due in part to the actions of others in the group (e.g. causing exclusion through deliberate poor passing which is then used to excuse ridiculing peers) – the interactions appear to be being set up for these purposes. Potentially nothing to do with the subject itself. Identify where appearing in diaries.

Certainly, at this point, the reflections were raising questions rather than answering them, and in doing so guided what followed. They therefore formed part of the hermeneutic processes involved here, i.e. informing interpretation (Zimmerman, 2015). What this did was give me a focus on looking at the interactions of the young people and how this impacted on engagement in their education. So, essentially, this was a process of identifying factors external to myself that appeared to be impacting on participants. Reflections can also include recording methodological decisions, key events and other factors that may have an impact on the quality and pathway of your research (Freeman & Mathison, 2008). Essentially, what you are doing through reflection is documenting the research process and responding purposefully to events as they arise.

Therefore, reflecting on what you see going on within the school environment can help with the focus of elements of your research in conjunction with your creative tools and identify features that tell you about the relationship between the two, and can help with your interpretation. What you will also benefit from doing is deepening your reflections to include consideration of the way you yourself may have influenced your research environment (for example, through the relationships you establish with children as based on your pre-existing values). In creative processes, this can become crucial in determining real depth to your work and involves the meaningful process of reflexivity (Everley and Flemons, 2020). A starting point for reflexive behaviours in research is the identification of the assumptions being made in the selection of research topics, which can include cultural assumptions about what is good for children – such as the white assumption that student-centred teaching necessarily addresses issues of social justice in education (Brannick & Coghlan, 2006).

Being reflexive is a particular feature of qualitative research and, because of the subject matter, creative enquiry. The importance of this is further magnified when conducting research with children. Earlier chapters discussed positionality and the beliefs/values that you hold as a researcher. Essentially speaking, reflexivity involves the actions that we take in response to this; to scrutinise what you do as a researcher in order to understand the impact this has on the research. Although there is a close relationship between reflection and reflexion (see, for example,

Morati, 2015), the two are distinct. When we discuss reflection, we are referring to the examination of the relationship between data and conclusions, whereas with reflexion we are examining the self and the data. What this also, inevitably, involves is attention to the processes involved in conducting the research.

Gormally and Coburn (2014) describe reflexive processes as a means of mitigating against researcher values. Burnard refers to this as the 'me-search within re-search', and this involves cognitive, emotional and sensory resources (Kara, 2015). Reflexion should take place prior to starting your research process and then should characterise your actions as you go through and complete your project. It is useful to draw here on elements of autoethnography, wherein you locate yourself within your own socio-cultural experiences to identify what affects the way that you think as a researcher (Viramontes, 2012) and how your identity impacts on your research. One of the ways of achieving this could be through reflecting on how you have arrived at the point you are in terms of your professional development and creating an autobiographical representation of key individuals and experiences that have affected your thinking. These are similar to activities that are used in initial teacher training. These can, for example, take the form of a timeline, but could also be a more patchworked account of key events that have impacted on you (Everley and Flemons, 2020). Such activities can make explicit any potential bias that may be seen either in the research process and/or analysis and interpretation. Being reflexive acknowledges the complexities of research environments and allows us to make what has been implicit, explicit. Thinking about how this can ultimately be used, Figure 7.1 illustrates how you can identify factors that have influenced you and understand how this then rationalises what your orientation to the work is. This can help challenge your own thinking and, if appropriate, you may then re-evaluate what you think.

Challenging your own assumptions is probably the most difficult to achieve, but can be worked towards by immersing yourself in your research environment in order to understand the experiences of children in school. Hermeneutically, as identified here, we understand the world based on what we notice from experience – as part of this process, there is potential for a 'fusion of horizons'

Figure 7.1 Identifying and utilising assumptions through reflexive processes

where we can integrate what is unfamiliar to become familiar, and therefore develop our perceptions (Zimmerman, 2015).

Achieving this can incorporate a process of purposely disrupting your own thinking. Here, it is helpful to actively question your assumptions and how they can apply to the children or young people you are working with. This can be facilitated by the support of a peer or teachers who may be involved in your research. Asking a colleague or peer to play 'devil's advocate' and question what your beliefs are can be one way of doing this. Essentially, what you need to do is find ways of engaging with opposing views that take you through the process of discerning what aspects of your predispositions do and do not apply to the situation you are investigating.

Maintaining a systematic, conscious process to considering our own theoretical and cultural orientations towards both the research topic and the research environment supports our ability to be critically aware of the relationship between our 'selves' and our research (Brannick & Coghlan, 2006; McCaffrey & Edwards, 2015; Warburton, 2016). The world discloses itself to us based on the perspectives from which we view it (Zimmerman, 2015). Identifying what we notice and why we are noticing particular 'things' can help the deliberate process of reflexion. Incorporating reflexive notes in your research diary can help with recording ongoing sense-making for you during your research (Konecki, 2019; Skains, 2018) and forms an essential part of this process.

There are many authors who are able to represent a comprehensive account of reflexive notes they have maintained as part of their research (see, for example, McCaffrey & Edwards, 2015). The stages of building the notes that I have spoken about in earlier chapters follows a pattern of, first, making what may be reflective notes and then revisiting them in order to build in a kind of meta-narrative, adding reflexive thoughts. You may find it helpful to consider your own notes of reflection and reflexion to be a 'live documentary' that is continually evolving and being reformed as you learn new things about your participants, research topic and yourself. Therefore, the maintenance of a research diary can extend to form a purposeful element of this process.

This can also help support you in dealing with the extensive uncertainties, discussed earlier in this text, associated with the unpredictable environments of school (Flanagan, 2012). This develops your sensitivity to the research environment and helps prevent a sense of failure when your research design needs adjusting.

One thing that may be helpful in getting you started in the process of including yourself constructively in the research is to ask a set of reflexive questions (Kara, 2015; Leibowitz et al., 2017). The box below makes some suggestions as to questions you may ask yourself in order to help orientate your process of reflexion prior to embarking on the research process:

> **Thinking points**
>
> Answering these questions can help you locate your identity within the research – the beginnings of reflexion:
>
> What is your own experience of the 'research topic'?
> Did you experience this topic as a child? (If so, how?)
> What led to your selection of the research topic?
> What meaning does this have for you?
> What does addressing the research question mean for you personally?
> What does addressing the research question mean for you professionally?
> How might you be different once you have addressed the research question(s)?

A good way of considering how you might answer these questions is through using the tools that you are asking your participants to engage with. This process can therefore serve the purpose of sensitising yourself to the research method, but also serve as exposition of pre-existing orientations as reflexion. Although they may have different cultural meanings to you, this may help with understanding this process and highlight what you really think about the topic.

Being reflexive is not just a way of making explicit your own orientations and therefore adding to the perceived 'truthfulness' of the research, but it can add to the quality of your interpretation. We can think about reflexion as being a process of writing yourself in and out of the research. Figure 7.2 illustrates how the purpose of reflexion works within the frame of acknowledging what preconceptions you may bring to the research and carry with you through it,

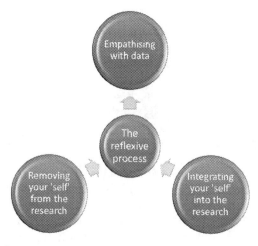

Figure 7.2 The reflexive process

and how identifying these may help in questioning these and separating yourself from what you are 'seeing' in the data. Thinking about how these points might be actively utilised allows you to empathise with the data. By empathising here, I refer to combining processes of attempting to adopt the perspective of the participants you are working with, but then stepping back to ensure that the data selected is conveying what you think as an ongoing process.

This process can help you locate yourself within your own research – to openly establish what you think about your research topic and how this might affect the way in which you engage in the process. This can serve two quite different, but related, purposes; the first being to identify how you might be restricted in what you may see in your 'data', in order to reduce this impact, or, second, to acknowledge your own orientation and openly explore how this affects your engagement, in celebration of this. This enables you to acknowledge how your questioning, interpretation and action all affect the way in which perspectives are shared by children. Essentially, reflexion is part of an ongoing analysis advocated by researchers working with young participants (Freeman & Mathison, 2008; Gormally & Coburn, 2014). Consulting with reflexive notes will inform such data analysis as an ongoing process (McCaffrey & Edwards, 2015). Maintaining a research journal can support the recording of role and identity in research, and can provide an overview of researcher role and identity (Konecki, 2019).

The practicalities of reflection and reflexion

Considering reflection and reflexion to be of value means that these factors will be integrated into your work. Having suggested journaling and maintaining field notes as ways of recording both, it is perhaps helpful now to discuss how you 'notice' what is significant in the research environment as you engage in it.

Mannay, Staples and Edwards (2017) advocate making the 'familiar strange' in order to take time to step back and really notice what we see going on in any situation. Being prepared to question your own approach can facilitate the process of ensuring that it is your participants that you are representing (rather than your existing opinions). A key thing to remember here is that it is perfectly acceptable to find that what you thought 'was the case', simply was not. It also addresses the kinds of concerns that some authors have expressed with regard to researcher subjectivities (Swartz, 2011). Being genuinely open to finding out something new requires us to make the familiar unfamiliar at the start of, and throughout, the research process. By virtue of the fact that you are selecting to investigate education, you will necessarily have a pre-existing interest in the topic you have chosen and, whilst this will positively inform the process you engage in, it is important that this does not prejudice you to what you are 'seeing'. This may also help refine your research question. An example of this could be if you were investigating the nature of gender and engagement in education. For example, there is a plethora of research that indicates girls and boys engage in education differently (Hamilton & Roberts, 2017; Hamilton & Jones, 2016). This I was finding to be the case with reference to children's drawings about their activities in free time within school. However, during informal engagement with these children (I spent a number of days with the class during their learning activities), one of them said 'it's fine because I have long hair so people sometimes think I'm a girl'. This got me thinking about how gender was being played out in the class – or how the processes of gendering were being implemented within the school. In turn, this made me return to some of the drawings that the children had made, to reconsider the gender indicators that existed within them and made me think beyond a binary approach to evaluating children's experiences in schools.

Using observations such as this is another way of disrupting your thinking, as previously discussed. Perhaps using some of the questions identified earlier in this chapter, you may find it helpful to follow the process below, which involves making the implicit, explicit and then questioning this. It will involve you thinking about what you think you know and why you think you know it (Kara, 2015).

Throughout whichever process you select to ensure reflection and reflexion in your research, it will nevertheless be important that your purpose remains focused on seeking as close a representation of your participants as possible, not to become embroiled in your 'self' (Greenbank, 2003) but to acknowledge how you are integrated into the research and make sense of your 'self' in the context of the research (Gormally & Coburn, 2014; Skains, 2018). It will also assist in challenging assumptions within the status quo that you may be seeking in your work (Gormally & Coburn, 2014).

The axiology of research tool selection

The concept of axiology (axios – worth, and logos – reason) is essentially the theory of values (Viega, 2016). Questioning your own values that are underpinning your actions can ensure that you are either consistent with those that you claim to have and/or that you ensure an alignment between these and your tool selection.

One of the things that it is very important to ensure is really where your philosophical stance is in terms of why you want to investigate a topic that concerns the experiences of children. Throughout this book, the focus is obviously on how there is an alignment between your epistemological beliefs and your ontological stance that informs your research tool selection – in other words, what you feel you need to know and how you might come to know this. In this case, how children experience the world and how best to understand this.

If you are reading this, you are likely to be researching for an undergraduate or postgraduate thesis, and a large part of your motivation will be to achieve success in your studies. If you are part of a research team, your goal will probably be to meet the needs of your funder and/or get your work published. If you are a practicing teacher, you may also have an enhanced awareness of the impact that your research will have on your own professional engagement as you move forward. However, it is also important to consider the impact that your research will have on the children you are working with, and there is an ethical requirement to consider the value that taking part in your study will have for your participants.

Swartz (2011) describes this as the 'intentional ethics of reciprocation'. Within the context of educational research, or any research that is conducted in a school setting, this can operate on the levels of children gaining some kind of benefit for taking part, which may be through understanding their own lived experiences or, perhaps, benefiting more indirectly through the impact that the research may have on the practices of their school (or other educational setting), or both. The nature of this may well depend on a number of factors, such as the age of the children you are working with and the openness of the school to responding to your findings. Researching physical activity and health within schools can lead to some changes in practice in terms of the free play opportunities offered to children but also be used as an opportunity to engage in discussion of health behaviours. It may be possible to link your work with particular learning activities that the school is engaged with – in the case just mentioned, perhaps a 'healthy living week' where research could serve to inform planning through gaining an understanding of children's existing health behaviours.

An essential factor is to ensure that you are transparent about the judgements you make during the research process, and this can be achieved through the reflexive processes identified above, thus linking to the axiology that underpins your work and which will potentially reveal unspoken realities with respect to your research question (Viega, 2016).

Ethical considerations

Your own values as a researcher will inevitably inform the considerations that you make when engaging in ethical approval processes (Greenbank, 2003). There is, however, a need to maintain an awareness throughout your work that can be informed through processes of sensitisation, reflection and reflexion. This establishes a basis for continued assurances that the research is of benefit to all involved (Collier, 2019). Understanding the complexities of ethical considerations of research with children necessarily requires engagement in reflexive processes (Sendil & Sonmez, 2020). Within this, you will be exposing any unconscious bias that you may have when considering how the research is impacting on your participants, thus helping in being ethically minded (Graham, Powell, & Taylor, 2015).

The purposeful integration of reflection and reflexion into your research practice supports the ethical basis on which you can critically evaluate the impact of your study on all involved, including yourself (Graham et al., 2015). In research with children, it is acknowledged that some dilemmas are highly complex, and attract no simple solutions. When such situations occur, depths of reflection are required to seek and apply appropriate solutions that minimise harm (Mortari & Harcourt, 2012).

Essentially, these processes underpin a continuing ethical awareness. This is particularly important as asking children to engage in research as competent social actors may, in itself, provide some ethical dilemmas for your own participants in terms of how they are able to embrace an approach that may be new to them (Freeman & Mathison, 2008). Being aware of how your children and young people are responding to all aspects of your work can support the ethical basis of your study, and through these processes the children themselves may help in guiding your strategies (Swartz, 2011). Essentially, the 'hallmark' of ethical agency is continuous and competent reflection and reflexion, involving both cognitive and emotional engagement (Mortari & Harcourt, 2012).

Conclusion

This chapter has considered how we can become sensitised to the research environment and be productively reflective and reflexive, considering the value set that we bring to studies with children. There is a need to identify and interrogate our own assumptions, and to write our 'selves' into our research. In order to achieve this effectively, we need to be unafraid to highlight uncertainties so that they can be addressed in light of what we are seeking to achieve. To do this, it is necessary to engage in reflexive questioning and to employ internal and external lenses in our work to step in and out of the research.

The discussion here has highlighted the value of engaging with the research tools that you are planning to use with your participants. This ensures that you not only understand the practicalities of that research tool but how it may feel to respond to a research question in this way, thus creating an empathy with your participants. It also enables you to create a depth of consciousness that explores the way in which your tool(s) may represent meaning, and the efficacy of this.

Thinking about how your own subjectivities can impact on your research helps mitigate against your skewing your data set. Attending to the need to review your positionality, and how this develops dynamically during your study, helps in finding and acknowledging your place in the process. Stepping into and out of the research helps in the processes of challenging your own thinking and sensitising yourself to your topic as experienced by your participants.

You should now have an understanding that:

Engaging in sensitising processes can enhance the clarity with which you employ particular research tools, ensuring purposeful requests
As a researcher, being reflexive makes you more aware of the ways in which you are affecting participants on a personal level

Being reflexive can attune you more specifically to the sensitivities and complexities of the research and enable you to make responsive ethical decisions during the research process

This book has endeavoured to provide you with a practical guide to researching using creative approaches in school contexts. An argument for such a text was established on the basis of the aligned evolution of research with children and visual research, but the absence of a particular set of pragmatic principles on which to design a study.

It began by defining what we mean by creative approaches and how these can be manifest in the design process, in our thinking as a creative researcher and in the utilisation of creative tools as both process and product. It considered how creativity can encompass a whole orientation of thinking in relation to research. Issues of engaging participants and generating rich data were explored, underpinning the more explicit exploration of particular research tools.

A range of research tools have been explored, along with their relative merits, as has the establishment of the need to carefully consider the individual preferences and needs of children as participants. Forms of representations through drawings, mapping, diagramming techniques or graphic elicitation have been discussed, as have photographs, video and generation of 3-D artefacts. These have value in themselves as representative of meaning, but also act as dynamic representations of children as they take part in research processes. Such dynamism is also evident over time as participants keep diaries or similar to record experiences in 'real time', adding different dimensions to understanding perspectives.

The need to ensure that the data that is generated through the use of such research tools is viable for analysis has also been discussed. Understanding how the process of producing material artefacts is affected by factors such as the intended audience, the presence of others and the environment in which they are created, all impact on the quality of data that results. The need to clarify meaning through narrative construction and framing by observational data is established as part of the iterative process of creative research.

The negotiation and application of concepts of power create an interactive basis upon which the multifarious relationships that exist within research in schools is applied to working with vulnerable participants and, perhaps, researching sensitive topics. The equivocal concept of empowerment has been explored in relation to the extent to which children can take control of aspects of the research process and of the interpretation of data with a sense of acknowledging this as relational and continually evolving.

Such distributions of power affect not only data generation but interpretation, and issues associated with the analysis of data have been explored in relation to establishing a rigorous approach to interrogating the artefacts that children produce and the context within which they have produced them. A need for a continual process of verification has been advocated from a constructivist perspective upon which clear understanding is established. The potential for wholly creative conclusions to be drawn are identified in relation to the possibilities of researchers generating a final creative interpretation of their participants' data.

The ultimate consideration of creative research with children in school contexts as an essentially reflective and reflexive process has been discussed. This has advocated for a conscious sensitisation to the tools, environments and relationships involved in research, emphasising the need recognise and forefront the subjectivities of this.

What should have been established within this text is an understanding of methodology that has been considered largely absent, or limited, in publications about researching with children (Allan & Tinkler, 2015). The exploration of ways of genuinely coming to understand children's perspectives and the meaning they apply to experience ensures a movement away from a reinforcement of pre-existing conceptions, to open up new possibilities in challenging the status quo. The centralisation of children's voices discussed here can be utilised in the generation of new theories and to challenge the tenets of those that already exist. This is achieved through creative thinking as a researcher across your approach to your subject of study.

Based on the assumption that you will be taking an emic epistemological stance in your work to understand children's experiences, this text has explored ways of understanding the complexity of children's experiences, which guide their responses to changing environments and support predicting future behaviour that may arise where there is a change as a result of research.

The means through which such experience can be understood have been presented as needing to be reflective of children's culture and sensory representations. A presentation of the need to privilege different ways of conveying meaning in research has been made, which is consistent with a wider shift of methods considered appropriate to understanding subjectivities.

Taking a pragmatic approach, the examples utilised here as illustrations are all taken from work in the field. The intention has been not to delimit what is likely to be achieved, but to generate examples that might open up your thinking in terms of the possibilities that this approach may have for you. On this basis, the text has also sought to discuss how research with children can be conducted within schools, not simply as locations of convenience but as environments that give a specific sense of 'place' to your work on a social, cultural and physical basis.

As a whole, this text has aimed to support you in thinking creatively in your approach, method selection and analysis; to view the school setting as socially constructed in the way it frames your work and affects the power relations that are enacted in order to establish a genuine understanding of what constitutes children's voices.

References

Allan, A., & Tinkler, P. (2015). 'Seeing' into the past and 'looking' forward to the future: visual methods and gender and education research. *Gender & Education*, 27(7), 791–811. doi:10.1080/09540253.2015.1091919.

Brannick, T., & Coghlan, D. (2006). Reflexivity in management and business research: what do we mean? *Irish Journal of Management*, 27(2), 143–160.

Collier, D. R. (2019). Re-imagining research partnerships: thinking through 'co-research' and ethical practice with children and youth. *Studies in Social Justice*, 13(1), 40–58. doi:10.26522/ssj.v13i1.1926.

Culshaw, S. (2019). The unspoken power of collage? Using an innovative arts-based research method to explore the experience of struggling as a teacher. *London Review of Education*, 17(3), 268–283. doi:10.18546/LRE.17.3.03.

Everley, S., & Flemons, M. (2021). 'Exploring and understanding your own experiences as a physical education teacher' (pp. 54–70) in S. Capel, J. Cliffe and J. Lawrence (Eds) *Learning to Teach Physical Education in Secondary School*, 5th Ed. London and New York: Routledge.

Fautley, M., & Savage, J. (2007). *Creativity in Secondary Education*. Exeter: Learning Matters.

Flanagan, P. (2012). Ethical review and reflexivity in research of children's sexuality. *Sex Education*, 12(5), 535–544. doi:10.1080/14681811.2011.627731.

Fletcher, G. (2013). Of baby ducklings and clay pots: method and metaphor in HIV prevention. *Qualitative Health Research*, 23(11), 1551–1562. Retrieved from http://search.ebscohost.com/login.aspx?direct=true&db=edsbl&AN=RN351780070&site=eds-live.

Freeman, M., & Mathison, S. (2008). *Researching Children's Experiences*. New York: Guilford Publications.

Gormally, S., & Coburn, A. (2014). Finding Nexus: connecting youth work and research practices. *British Educational Research Journal*, 40(5), 869–885. doi:10.1002/berj.3118.

Graham, A., Powell, M. A., & Taylor, N. (2015). Ethical research involving children: encouraging reflexive engagement in research with children and young people. *Children & Society*, 29(5), 331–343. doi:10.1111/chso.12089.

Greenbank, P. (2003). The role of values in educational research: the case for reflexivity. *British Educational Research Journal*, 29(6), 791–801. doi:10.1080/0141192032000137303.

Hamilton, P., & Roberts, B. (2017). 'Man-up, go and get an ice-pack.' Gendered stereotypes and binaries within the primary classroom: a thing of the past? *Education 3–13*, 45(1), 122–134.

Hamilton, P. L., & Jones, L. (2016). Illuminating the 'boy problem' from children's and teachers' perspectives: a pilot study. *Education 3–13*, 44(3), 241–254.

Hammershoj, L. G. (2014). Creativity in education as a question of cultivating sensuous forces. *Thinking Skills and Creativity*, 13, 168–182. doi:10.1016/j.tsc.2014.05.003.

Kara, H. (2015). *Creative Research Methods in the Social Sciences – A Practical Guide*. Bristol: Policy Press.

Konecki, K. T. (2019). Creative thinking in qualitative research and analysis. *Qualitative Sociology Review*, 15(3), 6–25. doi:10.18778/1733-8077.15.3.01.

Leibowitz, B., Bozalek, V., Farmer, J., Garraway, J., Herman, N., Jawitz, J., ... Winberg, C. (2017). Collaborative research in contexts of inequality: the role of social reflexivity. *Higher Education: The International Journal of Higher Education Research*, 74(1), 65. doi:10.1007/s10734-016-0029-5.

Lynch, C. (2008). Reflexivity in research on civil society: constructivist perspectives. *International Studies Review*, 10(4), 708.

Mannay, D., Staples, E., & Edwards, V. (2017). Visual methodologies, sand and psychoanalysis: employing creative participatory techniques to explore the educational experiences of mature students and children in care. *Visual Studies*, 32(4), 345–358.

McCaffrey, T., & Edwards, J. (2015). Meeting art with art: arts-based methods enhance researcher reflexivity in research with mental health service users. *Journal of Music Therapy*, 52(4), 515–532. doi:10.1093/jmt/thv016.

Mortari, L., & Harcourt, D. (2012). 'Living' ethical dilemmas for researchers when researching with children. *International Journal of Early Years Education*, 20(3), 234–243. doi:10.1080/09669760.2012.715409.

Sendil, Ç. O., & Sonmez, S. (2020). Ethics in research including young children: views and experiences of researchers. *Ilkogretim Online*, 19(1), 87–99. doi:10.17051/ilkonline.2020.644821.

Skains, R. L. (2018). Creative practice as research: discourse on methodology. *Media Practice & Education*, 19(1), 82–97. doi:10.1080/14682753.2017.1362175.

Swartz, S. (2011). 'Going deep' and 'giving back': strategies for exceeding ethical expectations when researching amongst vulnerable youth. *Qualitative Research*, 11(1), 47–68. doi:10.1177/1468794110385885.

Thomas, G. (1998). The Myth of Rational Research. *British Educational Research Journal*, 24(2), 141–162.

Viega, M. (2016). Science as art: axiology as a central component in methodology and evaluation of arts-based research (ABR). *Music Therapy Perspectives*, 34(1), 4–13.

Viramontes, A. (2012). Autoethnographic reflections: autoethnography as a signature pedagogy of speech communication. *Transformative Dialogues: Teaching & Learning Journal*, 6(1), 1–10.

Warburton, T. (2016). Turning the lens: reflexivity in research & teaching with critical discourse analysis. *Critical Questions in Education*, 7(3), 249–267.

Zimmerman, J. (2015). *Hermeneutics – A Very Short Introduction*. Oxford: Oxford University Press.

Index

Note: Page locators in *italic* refer to figures.

Adey, P. 6, 56
Anderson, J. 6, 56, 61, 62
anonymity, protecting 11, 50–51, 104
Arnott, L. 8, 10, 25, 26, 66, 83
assumptions 98–99, 111; challenging of own 112–113, *112*, 115
'audiences' 34–35, 51, 59, 95, 97
autoethnography 112
axiology of research tool selection 116–117

benefits to children of taking part in research 22, 31, 79, 117
Bevan, P. 6
Blaisdell, C. 8, 66, 83
blogging 18, 49
Braun, V. 101

cameras 40
Chesworth, L. 22, 31, 43, 64, 83, 89
children's consent 10–11, 26, 67, 83
Clark, A. 3, 4, 5, 22
Clarke, V. 101
clay-like materials 44–45, *46*
coding and categorizing data 101–102
collage and 3-D representations of meaning 44–47, *45*, *46*, *47*
colours 95
consent 9–11, 83; children's 10–11, 26, 67, 83; parental/guardian 9–10, 83, 84
creative approach to research 14–29; creative thinking 16–17, *17*; defining 15–16; effectiveness 27; engaging participants 17–23; ethical considerations 25–26; rich data generation 23–25, *23*
creative thinking 16–17, *17*, 27, 51, 109

culture, children's 21–22, 26, 27, 34, 40, 49, 51–52, 65

data, generation of viable 55–70; audience, people and place 59–61; children's control over 26; creative tools and rich data 23–25, *23*; credibility of data 58–59; defining viable data 55–59, 68; ensuring product viability 56, *56*; ethical considerations 66–67; generating narratives 65–66, 92; integrating narrative indicators 64–65; recording additional information 64; sense of place in situating material artefacts 61–64; trustworthiness of data 58, 59; validity and reliability of data 57–58
data interpretation and analysis 88–107; avoiding making assumptions 98–99; checking validity 66, 82, 93, 99, 102; coding and categorizing 101–102; creative methods of 100–101; data set analysis 91–100; empowerment and ownership of data 81–82; environmental factors 95; ethical considerations 103–104; indexical links 94, 96; inviting children to verify 102; meaning of 88–90; mismatches between aspects of data 99–100; overall process 102–103, *103*; temporal location of data 95, 98; theming 101–102; utilising researcher-recorded data 90–91; working with another researcher or a teacher 102
data sets 91–100, *91*; model for analysis of children's 92, *93*; objectivity and subjectivity 96–97; presentation of content 95–97, *96*, *97*; process of generating

92, *92*; understanding presentation of content 98–100; who and what is being represented 92–95
diagramming 35, 100
diaries, children's 20, 48–50, 55; choice of space for discussion of 62–63; drawings and added words 5, 18–19, *18, 19*; meta-narratives 64–65
diaries, research 113, 115
digital cameras 40
digital messaging 49
disposable cameras 40
divergent thinking 16–17, 27, 51, 109
drawings: ability to convey meaning through 65–66; analysis of children's 93, 94, *94*, 95–96, *96*, *97*; gender indicators in 116; graphic elicitation 36; maps and diagrammatic tools 35, *35*; metaphor in 33–34, *34*; potential 'audience' for 34–35; presentation 96, *97*; as a research tool 32–35; sensitisation to research tool of 108–109; words and relating the two 5, 18–19, *18, 19*, 33–35

Edwards, J. 4, 6, 21, 25, 30, 57, 58, 100, 113, 115
Edwards, V. 5, 31, 74, 89, 115
'emic' and 'etic' perspectives in research 5, 120
empathy, developing skills of 108–109
empowerment: contested nature of 78–80; ownership of interpretation and 81–82; in research process 80–81, *81*
engagement of children with research 17–23
environment for research: appropriate choice of location 61–64; to support self-expression of children 59–61; unpredictability of school 6–7, 61–62, 113
ethical approval 8–11
ethical considerations: in creative approach to research 25–26; in data interpretation and analysis 103–104; in generating viable data 66–67; in power relations 82–85; research sensitivities and reflections 117–118; selecting tools for creative research 50–51
Everley, K. 62
Everley, S. 2, 4, 62, 89, 93, 101, 110, 111, 112

'everyday' experiences, photo-elicitation and 36–37
experience, sharing of researcher's 74

Fautley, M. 16, 17, 18, 19, 21, 109
field notes 64, 66, 90–91, 110–111, 115
Flemons, M. 110, 111, 112
Foucault, M. 71, 79

gendering process implementation in schools 116
Giguere, M. 5, 45, 101–102
Gordon, C. 71, 78
graphic elicitation 36
Gravestock, H. 109
Guba, E. 2, 5, 58

Hammershoj, L.G. 14, 16, 18, 23, 25, 102, 109
Hilppö, J. 3, 30, 59, 89
humour, sharing of 75

incentives to take part in research 84–85
indexical links 94, 96
'intelligent noticing' 92, 110
interviews with children 62–63, 66, 98–99, 101, 102; children's control of 80, 81, 84; as data analysis and generation 92; group 37; photo-elicitation 36; working with specialist school staff 75

journals *see* diaries, children's; diaries, research

Kara, H. 15, 16, 25, 31, 33, 35, 38, 43, 47, 48, 58, 88, 100, 101, 108, 110, 112, 113, 116
knowledge: acquisition 5–6; creative methods and generation of 4–5; extraction and creation 22–23; power and production of 71

language, representation of and through 104
Lincoln, Y.S. 2, 5, 57, 58
Lipponen, L. 3, 4, 19, 20, 21, 22, 30, 31, 38, 40, 59, 89, 102
looked after children 83
Luttrell, W. 37, 38, 40, 41, 88, 99, 102, 104

Macfadyen, T. 89, 101
Mann, R. 24, 31, 88, 100

Mannay, D. 5, 31, 45, 74, 77, 79, 89, 93, 115
mapping 35, *35*, 100
Martinez-Lejarreta, L. 8, 25, 66, 83
McCaffrey, T. 4, 6, 21, 25, 30, 57, 58, 100, 113, 115
meta-narratives 64–65
metaphor: in drawings 33–34, *34*; in photographs 41, *41*
micro-blogging 49
mismatches between aspects of data 99–100
montage 100
mood, conveying of 94, 95, 96
music 30, 100

narratives, generating 65–66, 92

objects of importance to children 94, *94*

Paananen, M. 3, 19, 30, 59, 80
Palaiologou, I. 8, 25, 66, 83
parental/guardian consent 9–10, 83; refusal 84
pets 94
photographs: accessibility of spaces to take 42; adding captions 41; altering and enhancing 39, *39*; analysis of children's 93; digital sharing of 42–43; ethical considerations 50; metaphor 41, *41*; peer group audiencing 37; photo-elicitation 36–37; photo-voice 38–39; practicalities of using 40–43; presentation 95–96, *96*; single snapshots or series of images 38–39
place: audience, people and 59–61; sense of place in situating material artefacts 61–64
plasticine and play doh 44, 74
poems 47, 49, 100
positionality of researcher 75, 89, 118
power relations 71–87; between children 76–77; contested nature of empowerment 78–80; empowerment in research process 80–81, *81*; ethical considerations 82–85; ownership of data interpretation 81–82; sensitive subjects 77–78, 85; vulnerable groups 72–77, *73*
preparation phase of research 89–90

presentation of data 95–97, *96*, *97*; understanding 98–100
privacy of participants 104
pseudonyms 104

qualitative research, quality criteria for 58

Rajala, A. 3, 19, 30, 59, 89
reflection 22–23, 102; practicalities of 115–116; purpose of 110–111
reflexion: practicalities of 115–116; process of 114–115, *114*; purpose of 111–115, *112*
relational self 98
relationships, representations of 94, 95–97, *96*, *97*
research with children 3–4
rewards for taking part in research 84–85

safeguarding 50–51, 78
sandbox scenes 45–47, *47*
Sanderud, J.R. 3, 38, 39, 42, 43
Savage, J. 16, 17, 18, 19, 21, 109
school environment, unpredictable 6–7, 61–62, 113
SEND children, working with 74, 75
sensitising of researcher 108–122; axiology of research tool selection 116–117; ethical considerations 117–118; practicalities of reflection and reflexion 115–116; purpose of reflection and reflexion 110–115; sensitisation to research tools 108–109, 114, 118
sensitive topics: environment for discussion of 60–61; ethical considerations 67, 82, 84, 85; impact on researcher 85; researching 77–78; tools for exploring 36, 38
sharing of researcher's experience 74
size of groups 76–77
"slow listening" 89
smartphones 40
social maps 35, *35*
social media 21, 42–43, 49
space: accessibility of 42; appropriate choice of research 61–64; temporal aspects of 62
Staples, E. 5, 31, 74, 89, 115
suggestion boxes 83

Swartz, S. 4, 38, 71, 74, 78, 79, 82, 104, 115, 117, 118

terminology 7
theming data 101–102
Thomas, G. 92, 110
three dimensional representations of meaning 44–47, *45*, *46*, *47*
time maps 36
tools, creative: accessibility 21, 65; engaging participants 17–23; features of effective 19, *20*; involvement of researcher 20; malleability of 20–21, 24–25; rich data generation 23–25, *23*; sensitisation to research 108–109, 114, 118
tools, selection of creative 30–54; axiology of 116–117; children's input to 80–81; collage and 3-D representations of meaning 44–47; drawings 32–35; ethical considerations 50–51; graphic elicitation 36; maps and diagrammatic tools 35–36; photographs 36–43; types of visual expression 31–50; videos, use of 43–44; written research data 47–50
traveller communities 74

UN Convention on the Rights of the Child 4

values, theory of 116
Vaswani, N. 3, 4, 42, 67, 85
video, use of 43–44, 51
vignettes 47–48
visits to school/class prior to starting research 89–90
visual data as polysemic 65, 93–94
visual expression, types of 30–50; collage and 3-D representations of meaning 44–47; diaries and other forms of written expression 47–50; drawings 32–35, 32–36; maps and diagrammatic tools 35–36; photographs 36–43; video 43–44; video, use of 43–44; written research data 47–50; written research data and diaries 47–50
vulnerable groups 72–77, *73*

Wall, K. 8, 25, 66, 83
Warr, D. 18, 24, 31, 88, 100
written research data 47–50

Printed in the United States
by Baker & Taylor Publisher Services